The Data Powered Regional Bank

A Practical Guide for Implementation and Success in Artificial Intelligence

Tim Heaton

12-1-2023

ISBN: 9798870628820

Contents

Introduction

"The Data Powered Regional Bank" is a comprehensive guide aimed at unlocking the potential of Artificial Intelligence (AI) and Machine Learning (ML) in regional banking. This book provides an in-depth understanding of these technologies and their practical application in the banking sector. It serves as a strategic resource, aligning technological innovations with actionable strategies for digital transformation in regional banking, enriched with over thirty practical AI application recipes.

Author's Perspective and Experience: As the author, I bring extensive research and firsthand industry insights to this guide. My journey in the financial sector, enriched by interactions with industry experts and hands-on experience in implementing AI solutions, forms the foundation of this book. The knowledge and experiences gathered throughout my career are distilled here, offering readers a clear, concise, and step-wise path to integrating AI and ML in banking.

Context and Relevance: In the current fast-paced financial landscape, AI and ML are more than just industry buzzwords; they are critical drivers reshaping the banking sector. Regional banks are at a crossroads, facing challenges and opportunities brought on by rapid technological advancements. The demand for enhanced efficiency, superior customer service, and robust risk management has never been greater. AI and ML emerge as key solutions, providing innovative and transformative approaches that redefine banking in the modern era.

Author's Call for Collaboration: I encourage collaboration and am open to questions, suggestions, or discussions about potential partnerships. If you're interested in my work or would like to view some of my code developed in Python and SQL, please feel free to reach out to me at tim.h.heaton@gmail.com.

Chapter 1: Why Do It? Leveraging Your Natural Advantages

Regional Banks and Money Center Banks play distinct yet complementary roles in the financial ecosystem. Each serves unique functions and caters to different customer segments. Below is a comparison of their roles:

Regional Banks:

Client Base and Geographic Focus:

- Regional banks primarily serve a specific geographic area, focusing on local communities or regions.
- Their clientele generally includes individual consumers, local businesses, and small to medium-sized enterprises (SMEs).

Services Offered:

- These banks provide traditional banking services such as checking and savings accounts, mortgages, personal loans, and credit facilities, often tailored to local needs.
- While regional banks may offer wealth management and investment services, these are typically less extensive than those available at larger banks.

Community Involvement:

- Regional banks are known for their strong community ties and personalized service.
- They frequently engage in local development projects, playing a vital role in the financial well-being of the communities they serve.

Operational Scale and Innovation:

- Regional banks usually operate on a smaller scale compared to money center banks.
- They might have limited resources for extensive technological innovations but often exhibit greater agility in their decision-making processes.

Money Center Banks:

Client Base and Geographic Focus:

- Money center banks have a broad focus, catering to customers ranging from individuals to large corporations and governments, both nationally and internationally.
- Their services are designed to meet the diverse requirements of a global client base.

Services Offered:

- These banks offer a comprehensive range of services, including retail banking, wealth management, investment banking, international trade financing, and treasury services.
- They are significantly involved in high-volume, large-scale financial transactions.

Community Involvement:

- Money center banks may participate in community projects, but their larger scale often translates to less direct community involvement compared to regional banks.
- Their primary focus tends to be on global economic trends and large-scale development initiatives.

Operational Scale and Innovation:

- Operating on a much larger scale, money center banks maintain extensive branch and ATM networks across various regions or countries.
- They are often at the forefront of technological innovation in the banking sector, investing heavily in fintech and advanced digital banking services.

AI's Role in the Global Banking Experience:
- Artificial Intelligence (AI) and Machine Learning (ML) are crucial in enhancing the digital experience in banking, especially for money center banks.
- These technologies significantly improve customer interactions, fraud detection, operational efficiency, and risk management, profoundly influencing the banking landscape.

Contrasting Regional and Money Center Banks:

Scope and Scale:

- Regional banks focus on serving the needs of individuals and local businesses, emphasizing localized services. In contrast, money center banks operate on a national and international level, catering to a diverse client base including large corporations and governments.

Service Personalization:

- Known for their personalized customer service, regional banks maintain strong ties with their local communities. Money center banks, due to their larger size, may offer less personalization but compensate with a broader range of services.

Technological Advancements:

- Money center banks generally have more resources to invest in technological advancements, whereas regional banks often adhere to traditional banking practices. However, regional banks can be more agile and responsive to changes in local markets.

Economic Impact:

- The activities of money center banks significantly influence national and global economies. Regional banks, on the other hand, primarily contribute to local or regional economic development.

Regional banks, with their community-centric approach, cultivate deep customer-employee relationships and offer personalized services, fostering a sense of community belonging. Their geographical proximity to customers enables them to provide immediate, face-to-face problem-solving and tailored financial solutions, bolstering customer loyalty.

Cost and Economy of Scale in Banking:

- Money center banks benefit from economies of scale, which can lead to lower operating costs, a broader deposit base, and diversified revenue streams. Their access to capital markets is typically more robust, facilitating...
- Money center banks, with their economies of scale, enjoy benefits like lower operating costs, a broader deposit base, and diversified revenue streams. They have superior access to capital markets, which supports their investments in technology and global operations.
- However, the advent of Artificial Intelligence (AI) and Machine Learning (ML) provides regional banks with tools to bridge this gap. These technologies enable regional banks to enhance their efficiency and competitiveness despite their smaller scale.

Leveraging Your Bank's Natural Advantages with Artificial Intelligence
Advantage: AI for Enhanced Community Involvement

- In the digital era, regional banks are well-placed to use Artificial Intelligence (AI) to strengthen their community involvement. Historically, these banks have been integral to local economic development, forging strong relationships with residents and businesses. AI integration into their operations can further enhance these community connections, offering more personalized banking experiences and targeted community support. This section delves into how regional banks can employ AI to create highly customized applications for community involvement.

Understanding the Community-Centric Approach of Regional Banks

- Regional banks stand out due to their profound understanding and dedication to their local communities. Their ability to meet the unique needs of local customers, provide tailored financial advice, and support community initiatives has been key to their success. Adapting to the fast-paced digital environment while maintaining this level of personalized service is a challenge that requires technological innovation.

The Role of AI in Customizing Community Services

- AI's ability to process and analyze extensive data sets allows for the identification of trends, preferences, and specific needs within a community. By harnessing AI, regional banks can obtain valuable insights into local economic conditions, consumer behavior, and evolving community requirements. This knowledge is critical for the development of financial products and services that truly align with the needs and expectations of the local population.

AI-Driven Financial Inclusion Programs

- AI presents a significant opportunity in the development of financial inclusion programs. By analyzing demographic data, spending patterns, and financial behaviors, AI enables banks to identify underserved or unbanked segments within their communities. Consequently, banks can design services to address these specific needs, offering personalized credit options, financial literacy initiatives, and savings products for diverse population segments.

Customized Loan and Grant Programs

- The predictive capabilities of AI allow regional banks to provide more personalized loan and grant programs. Understanding the unique challenges faced by local businesses and residents, banks can develop specialized loan products with flexible terms tailored to their needs. AI also aids in pinpointing businesses and individuals who may benefit most from grants or low-interest loans, especially during economic downturns.

Enhancing Community Engagement Through AI-Enabled Platforms

- AI-driven platforms offer regional banks an innovative way to engage directly with their communities. These platforms can act as interactive forums where customers can express their concerns, propose initiatives, or participate in voting for community projects. AI's ability to analyze such feedback is instrumental in prioritizing community development endeavors and optimizing resource allocation.

Personalized Banking Experiences

- AI technologies such as chatbots and virtual assistants play a crucial role in enhancing customer service. They provide 24/7 support, answering queries and offering personalized financial advice. By learning from customer interactions, these AI tools are able to deliver more customized banking suggestions, thus improving overall customer satisfaction.

AI in Financial Education and Awareness Programs

- Regional banks can utilize AI to create and implement financial education programs specifically tailored to the needs of their communities. By analyzing local financial literacy levels, banks can develop customized educational content that addresses particular knowledge gaps. This approach empowers residents to make more informed financial decisions and enhances their financial well-being.

Localized Chatbots and Virtual Assistants:

- Developing AI-powered chatbots that comprehend and communicate in local dialects and languages can significantly improve the customer service experience. These chatbots can handle routine queries, manage account-related tasks, and provide instant assistance, all tailored to meet the specific banking needs of the local community.

Personalized Financial Advisory Services:

- AI can be leveraged to analyze an individual customer's financial data, offering personalized advice on savings, investments, and budget management.

- Implement AI-driven tools that provide custom investment recommendations, taking into account a customer's financial goals, risk tolerance, and local economic factors.

Predictive Analytics for Customer Needs:

- Utilizing predictive analytics, banks can anticipate customer needs based on life events, spending patterns, and financial behavior.
- This allows banks to proactively offer relevant products and services, such as pre-approved loans, insurance, or tailored investment options, at opportune times.

Enhanced Mobile Banking Experience:

- Integrating AI into mobile banking applications can introduce features like voice-activated commands, personalized alerts, and intelligent financial management suggestions.
- Develop an AI-driven, intuitive user interface in the banking app that adapts to each user's individual preferences and banking habits.

Community-Centric Product Recommendations:

- AI can help banks identify and comprehend the unique financial needs of the communities they serve.
- Based on this understanding, banks can offer customized banking products and services, such as special loans for local businesses, agricultural credits, or community development funds.

Fraud Detection and Security Alerts:

- Implementing AI algorithms enables quick detection of unusual account activity, providing real-time alerts to customers about potential fraud.
- Tailoring the fraud detection system to recognize common transaction patterns within the community not only enhances its effectiveness but also reduces false positives.

Financial Literacy and Education Programs:

- Developing AI-powered educational tools and apps can provide financial literacy resources, customized to the specific needs of the community.
- Offer interactive learning modules covering essential topics such as budgeting, saving, investing, and credit management, tailored to different levels of financial understanding and experience.

Sentiment Analysis for Customer Feedback:

- Utilizing AI for sentiment analysis of customer feedback across various channels, including social media, surveys, and direct customer interactions, can be highly beneficial.
- This analysis provides valuable insights into customer satisfaction and preferences, enabling banks to refine their services and communication strategies accordingly.

Customized Credit Scoring Models:

- Implementing AI-based credit scoring models that account for local economic conditions and alternative data sources can lead to more accurate risk assessments for community-based loan applicants.
- These models can offer a more holistic view of an applicant's financial health, especially beneficial in regions with diverse economic backgrounds.

Automated Account Handling and Queries:

- AI can be used to automate routine account management tasks, such as updating personal information, processing transactions, and addressing frequently asked questions.
- Ensuring that these automated systems are customized to the specific types of accounts and services prevalent among the bank's customer base will enhance efficiency and user satisfaction.

Advantages: Micro - Leveraging AI in Regional Banks

Regional banks possess distinct advantages due to their community-centric approach, personalized services, and intimate knowledge of local markets. The integration of Artificial Intelligence (AI) can amplify these strengths in several key areas:

Local Market Insights and Trend Analysis:

- AI can be used to analyze local economic data and trends, enabling banks to gain a nuanced understanding of the specific needs of their local markets and tailor services accordingly.
- This technology allows banks to predict and adapt to local economic shifts, such as changes in the housing market, regional employment trends, or local business growth, ensuring timely and relevant responses.

Customized Risk Assessment Models:

- Developing AI models that factor in local economic variables can lead to more precise credit and investment risk assessments tailored to the local clientele.
- These models enable banks to offer more advantageous loan terms and investment advice, grounded in a thorough understanding of local risk factors.

Community Engagement and Social Listening:

- AI-driven social listening tools can monitor and analyze community discussions on social media and online platforms.
- Insights gleaned from these conversations can guide the bank's community involvement and corporate social responsibility (CSR) initiatives, ensuring they are aligned with community concerns, interests, and needs.

Targeted Marketing and Product Development:

- AI can analyze customer data to pinpoint cross-selling and upselling opportunities, based on the banking behaviors and preferences of local customers.
- This enables the development and marketing of banking products and services uniquely designed for the local community, ensuring they are more closely aligned with their needs and expectations.

Enhanced Personalization in Banking Services:

- AI can be applied to personalize each customer's banking experience, offering tailored product recommendations, financial advice, and customer service.
- AI-driven personal finance tools can assist customers in managing their finances more effectively, providing insights and suggestions based on their financial habits and goals.

Optimized Branch Operations:

- AI can be utilized to analyze branch traffic and transaction patterns, allowing for the optimization of staffing and operational efficiency.
- Automating routine in-branch tasks frees up staff to focus on more personalized customer interactions, enhancing the overall customer experience.

Fraud Detection Specific to Local Patterns:

- Implementing AI systems designed to recognize fraud patterns and anomalies specific to the regional bank's customer base and transaction types can significantly improve security.
- This approach enhances fraud detection capabilities while ensuring the ease of doing business for local customers is not compromised.

AI-Enabled Customer Feedback and Resolution:

- AI can swiftly process and respond to customer feedback and complaints, leading to quicker resolution times and improved customer satisfaction.
- Continuous analysis of feedback through AI can guide ongoing improvements in products and services, ensuring they remain responsive to customer needs.

Employee Training and Development:

- AI can be utilized for personalized training and development programs for bank employees. This enhances their skills in areas most relevant to the local market and customer needs, improving service quality and market responsiveness.

By leveraging AI in these ways, regional banks can not only enhance their existing strengths but also create new avenues to serve their communities more effectively. This can lead to maintaining a competitive edge and fostering deeper customer loyalty.

Unique Challenges Regional Banks Face in Implementing AI:

Data Limitations:

- **Scale and Diversity:** Compared to larger banks, regional banks often work with smaller, less diverse datasets. This can impact the training and effectiveness of AI models, as AI systems generally require large and varied data sets to function optimally.
- **Quality and Integration:** Smaller banks may face challenges with data quality and integration. The lack of integrated data systems can pose significant hurdles for effective, data-driven AI applications.

Resource Constraints:

- **Financial and Technological Resources:** Regional banks often operate with limited budgets, which may restrict their ability to invest in advanced AI technologies or the necessary infrastructure.

- **Expertise:** Gaining access to AI expertise and talent is another significant challenge, particularly in smaller or more rural areas where regional banks are commonly located.

Customer Relationship Dynamics:

- Regional banks are celebrated for their personalized customer service. Integrating AI without compromising this human touch can be a delicate balance to maintain.
- Resistance from customers who prefer traditional banking methods and may be wary of AI-driven services is also a potential challenge.

Regulatory Compliance and Ethical Considerations:

- Navigating the complex regulatory landscape while implementing AI poses a significant challenge. Regional banks must stay compliant with both local and federal regulations, which can be particularly demanding with the constantly evolving nature of AI technologies.
- Ethical considerations in the use of AI are also paramount to maintain trust and integrity.

Technology Implementation and Integration:

- Integrating AI into existing legacy systems can be both challenging and expensive. Many regional banks operate with older infrastructures that may not seamlessly integrate with the latest AI technologies.
- Scaling AI solutions to fit the specific needs of the bank and ensuring their adaptability is another hurdle that needs careful planning and execution.

Cybersecurity Concerns:

- Ensuring robust cybersecurity for AI systems, which handle sensitive customer data, is crucial. Regional banks may find it challenging to implement advanced security protocols effectively due to resource constraints.

- The risk of AI systems being targeted by cyber threats necessitates continuous monitoring and updating of security measures, adding another layer of complexity.

Training and Adaptation:

- Training employees to work efficiently with AI systems represents a significant change management challenge, requiring resource investment and strategic planning.
- Adapting to AI-enhanced processes may necessitate a cultural shift within the organization, which can be difficult to manage and requires careful handling to ensure staff buy-in.

Market and Competitive Pressures:

- Regional banks face the challenge of keeping pace with larger institutions in AI innovation while maintaining their core value of personalized service.
- Differentiating their AI-driven services in an increasingly competitive and technology-driven market is another challenge, requiring innovative strategies to stand out.

Ethical Considerations:

- Regional banks must navigate a unique set of ethical challenges when implementing AI, arising from their close community ties, smaller scale, and localized customer base. Addressing these ethical concerns is vital to maintaining trust and integrity within the communities they serve.

Some key ethical challenges include:

- Ensuring the fairness and transparency of AI-driven decisions, especially in credit scoring and financial advisory services.
- Balancing the use of customer data for personalized services with the need to maintain privacy and confidentiality.
- Managing the potential impact of AI on employment within the bank and the broader community.
- Navigating the ethical use of AI in marketing and customer interaction to avoid manipulation or biased approaches.

Bias in AI Algorithms:

- AI systems are influenced by the data they are trained on. Regional banks, often working with limited or region-specific datasets, face the risk of these data sets being skewed, potentially leading to biased AI decision-making. This is particularly crucial in areas like credit scoring, lending practices, or customer service.
- It's essential to ensure that AI algorithms are fair and unbiased, especially in diverse communities, to prevent discrimination against any group. This requires careful monitoring and continuous adjustment of the algorithms to reflect fairness and inclusivity.

Data Privacy and Community Trust:

- The reputation of regional banks is often built on strong personal relationships and trust. The introduction of AI in managing personal and financial data brings forth significant privacy and security concerns.
- Protecting customer data against breaches and unauthorized use is paramount. Banks must maintain transparency in how AI systems use and protect customer data to preserve this trust.

Automated Decision-Making Transparency:

- Decisions made by AI, particularly those affecting customers' financial status or creditworthiness, need to be transparent and understandable. Customers deserve to know how such decisions are made.
- Regional banks have the responsibility to ensure that their AI systems are not opaque 'black boxes.' Customers should have access to clear, comprehensible explanations for any AI-driven decisions that affect them.

Impact on Local Employment:

- The ability of AI to automate tasks raises concerns about job displacement, a critical issue in smaller communities where the bank might be a major employer.
- Banks need to carefully consider the impact of AI on their workforce and the local job market. They should aim to balance the efficiency gains from AI with the potential social implications, such as job loss or changing skill requirements.

Ethical Use of Predictive Analytics:

- While predictive analytics can enhance banking services, there is a delicate balance between beneficial prediction and privacy invasion. For example, using spending patterns to predict financial distress or life events might be perceived as intrusive.
- Regional banks must judiciously use predictive analytics, ensuring they respect customer privacy and avoid overstepping boundaries.

Community-specific AI Applications:

- AI applications should be specifically tailored to meet the needs and uphold the values of the local community. Generic solutions may not be suitable due to the unique cultural and socio-economic characteristics of the bank's customer base.
- Ethical considerations are crucial in developing AI solutions that are not only relevant but also genuinely beneficial to the local community.

Managing AI-Driven Changes in Customer Relations:

- Introducing AI could change the traditional, personal engagement model that is a hallmark of regional banks. There is a risk that this personal touch, often a key differentiator for these banks, might be diluted.
- It's important for banks to find a balance in implementing AI technologies without undermining the personal customer relationships they are celebrated for.

Access and Digital Divide:

- A heavy reliance on AI and digital tools might unintentionally exclude customers who are not technologically proficient or lack access to digital banking services.
- It is ethically imperative for regional banks to ensure that AI-enhanced services are accessible and inclusive, taking into account the diverse demographic profile of their customers.

By addressing these challenges, regional banks not only adhere to ethical standards but also reaffirm their dedication to serving their communities with responsibility and integrity. The goal is to find a harmonious balance between utilizing AI for operational efficiency and preserving the trust and personal connections that define regional banking.

Conclusion: AI and ML as Catalysts for Digital Transformation

In a rapidly evolving global banking landscape, regional banks are increasingly recognizing the need to adapt and innovate. The advent of Artificial Intelligence (AI) and Machine Learning (ML) technologies presents a significant opportunity for these institutions to elevate their service offerings, enhance operational efficiency, and maintain competitiveness.

AI and ML: Redefining the Future of Banking

The banking sector is amidst a profound digital transformation, with AI and ML leading this shift. These technologies are not just augmenting existing banking systems; they are essential drivers of change, fundamentally reshaping the ways banks operate, engage with customers, and make strategic decisions. The integration of AI and ML is a critical step for banks to stay competitive and relevant in an increasingly digitalized world.

This section has explored how AI and ML are more than just technological upgrades; they are pivotal tools that can redefine the future of banking. By offering smarter, more efficient, and customer-centric solutions, AI and ML are instrumental in guiding banks through this era of digital transformation.

Chapter 2: Introduction to Machine Learning and Artificial Intelligence

What is Artificial Intelligence?

Definition and Types of Artificial Intelligence

Artificial Intelligence (AI) represents the simulation of human intelligence processes by computer systems. It is a significant field within computer science, dedicated to creating intelligent agents – systems capable of reasoning, learning, and acting autonomously. AI research has yielded effective techniques for a broad spectrum of applications, ranging from game playing to medical diagnosis.

Key Characteristics of AI include:

- **Learning and Adaptation:** AI systems have the capability to learn from data and adapt their behavior accordingly. This characteristic enables continuous performance improvement and the ability to generalize to new situations.
- **Reasoning and Problem Solving:** AI systems are equipped to reason about their environment and solve problems using various techniques, including search, planning, and decision-making methodologies.
- **Perception and Understanding:** Through sensors, AI systems can perceive the world and process the information received. This ability allows them to meaningfully interact with the physical world.

Promising Applications of AI:

- **Automation:** AI can automate tasks traditionally performed by humans, such as driving vehicles, diagnosing diseases, and handling customer service.
- **Decision Making:** In areas such as finance, healthcare, and criminal justice, AI has the potential to make more informed decisions than humans.
- **Creativity:** AI can also be used to generate creative outputs, including music, art, and literature.

Types of AI:

- **Narrow or Weak AI:** This type of AI is specialized for specific tasks, such as voice assistants or image recognition systems. It functions within a limited, predefined range or context and lacks the broader cognitive abilities of human intelligence.
- **General or Strong AI:** This is a theoretical concept that refers to a system with generalized human cognitive abilities. Such a system would be capable of intelligently solving a wide array of problems in a manner similar to humans, but it remains a concept and has not been achieved yet.

Machine Learning (ML):

- ML is a crucial subset of AI. It involves developing algorithms that enable computers to learn and make decisions from data. Unlike traditional programming that relies on specific instructions written by humans, ML allows systems to learn and improve from experience automatically.

Current Artificial Intelligence Used by Regional Banks:

- **Enhanced Customer Experience:** AI-driven tools like chatbots provide personalized customer support, while ML algorithms can deliver customized financial advice based on individual customer data.
- **Improved Risk Management:** ML models are proficient in analyzing large datasets to identify and mitigate risks, particularly in areas like credit scoring and fraud detection.
- **Operational Efficiency:** AI automation of routine tasks reduces manual labor, improves accuracy, and decreases operational costs.
- **Data-Driven Decision Making:** AI and ML enable banks to analyze extensive datasets, leading to more informed business decisions based on insights from customer data, market trends, and risk assessments.
- **Compliance and Security:** AI systems can continuously monitor transactions for suspicious activity and ensure adherence to the evolving regulatory landscape.

- **Innovative Products and Services:** ML algorithms can aid in the development of new banking products and services, catering to the changing needs of customers.

Machine Learning in Banking Today

Machine Learning (ML) is revolutionizing the banking industry by offering sophisticated solutions to complex problems. Here is a breakdown of the various applications of ML in banking currently:

The Types of ML Algorithms:

ML algorithms can be broadly categorized into three types:

1. Supervised Learning:
     - These algorithms learn from a set of labeled training data and aim to predict outcomes or labels for new, unseen data.
     - Common examples include:
          - **Linear Regression:** Used for regression problems where the goal is to predict a continuous value.
          - **Logistic Regression, Support Vector Machines (SVM), and Neural Networks:** Used for classification tasks where the goal is to categorize data into predefined classes.
2. Unsupervised Learning:
     - These algorithms deal with unlabeled data, identifying patterns or groupings in the data without any prior training.
     - Common methods include:
          - **Clustering (e.g., K-means Clustering):** Used to group data points together based on similarities.
          - **Association (e.g., Apriori Algorithm):** Used to find rules that describe relationships between variables in large datasets.

3. Reinforcement Learning:
    - In this paradigm, an agent learns to make decisions by performing actions in an environment and receiving feedback in the form of rewards or penalties.
    - Examples include **Q-learning** and **Deep Reinforcement Learning Algorithms**, where the learning process is guided by the outcomes of the actions taken, rather than being explicitly taught.

Unique Factors of AI to Consider

Continuous Improvement:

- The predictive nature of ML models allows for continuous learning and improvement. As they process more data over time, these models become more accurate in predicting outcomes, such as customer churn. This enables banks to constantly refine their retention strategies and adapt to changing customer behaviors.

Current Machine Learning Applications in Banking

1. Fraud Detection and Prevention:
    - ML algorithms analyze transaction data in real-time to identify unusual patterns that may indicate fraudulent activities.
    - These models can learn from historical fraud data, making them more effective in detecting and preventing fraud compared to traditional rule-based systems.
2. Credit Scoring and Risk Assessment:
    - ML models enhance creditworthiness assessments by analyzing a wide range of data, including credit history, transaction data, and social media activities.
    - They identify subtle patterns that may indicate credit risk, thereby improving risk assessment accuracy.
3. Personalized Banking Services:

- By analyzing customer data, ML algorithms can understand individual preferences and behaviors, leading to personalized banking experiences.
- Personalization can extend to website interfaces, mobile apps, and communication strategies.

4. Customer Service and Support:
   - AI-powered chatbots and virtual assistants, equipped with ML, offer 24/7 customer support, improving service efficiency and customer satisfaction.

5. Anti-Money Laundering (AML) and Regulatory Compliance:
   - ML aids in monitoring transaction data for potential money laundering activities and ensures compliance with regulatory requirements.

6. Predictive Analytics:
   - Banks use ML for predictive analytics in loan default prediction, market trend forecasting, and customer churn analysis.

7. Algorithmic Trading:
   - ML algorithms execute high-frequency trades based on market data analysis, identifying patterns and executing trades faster than human traders.

8. Operational Efficiency:
   - ML automates routine tasks like data entry and risk assessments, enhancing operational efficiency and resource allocation.

9. Customer Segmentation:
   - ML helps segment customers based on spending habits and transaction behaviors, aiding in targeted marketing and product development.

10. Wealth Management and Robo-advisors:
    - ML-driven robo-advisors offer personalized investment advice and portfolio management with minimal human intervention.

11. Cybersecurity:

- ML improves cybersecurity by detecting and responding to network threats in real-time, continuously learning from new security threats.
12. Document Analysis and Processing:
    - ML automates the processing of large volumes of unstructured data, such as legal documents, enhancing efficiency and accuracy.
    -

Cutting Edge of Machine Learning Applications in Banking
Automating Regulatory Compliance with AI Technologies

AI technologies are playing an increasingly vital role in automating and streamlining the complex processes associated with regulatory compliance in banking. This development is enhancing efficiency and accuracy in several key areas:

1. Data Management and Analysis:
   - AI systems excel in managing and analyzing vast volumes of data relevant to compliance.
   - They efficiently process transaction records, customer data, and other pertinent information to identify patterns or anomalies that may signal non-compliance.
   - This capability not only aids in maintaining regulatory compliance but also helps in detecting potential risks or fraudulent activities.
2. Real-Time Monitoring:
   - AI tools are crucial for real-time monitoring of banking operations, an essential component in ensuring continual compliance.
   - These systems are capable of rapidly adapting to changes in regulatory landscapes. Whether there are updates to anti-money laundering laws, changes in cross-border transaction rules, or adjustments in financial reporting standards, AI systems can adjust almost instantaneously.

- This real-time adaptability ensures that the bank remains compliant and up-to-date with all regulatory changes, reducing the risk of non-compliance penalties.

The integration of AI into regulatory compliance processes signifies a significant shift in how banks manage and respond to regulatory requirements. By leveraging AI for data analysis and real-time monitoring, banks can navigate the complex and ever-changing regulatory environment more effectively and efficiently. AI is transforming traditionally labor-intensive and error-prone processes into streamlined, reliable operations.

Steps Involved in the ML Process

The Machine Learning (ML) process in a banking environment involves a series of critical steps, each contributing to the success of ML projects:

Step One: Data Collection Data forms the foundation of any ML model. The data collection step is about gathering a comprehensive and relevant dataset for the model to learn from. In a banking context, finding pertinent data for ML projects requires navigating both technical and organizational challenges. Here are some strategies for sourcing relevant data:

1. **Understand the Business Problem:** Start with a clear understanding of the business issue or objective the ML project is targeting. This clarity will direct you to the types of data that will be most beneficial.
2. **Consult with Domain Experts:** Engage with banking professionals with expertise in areas like risk management, customer service, or finance. They can provide insights on available data and its potential applications.

3. **Identify Internal Data Sources:** Investigate internal data sources, including transaction databases, customer profiles, loan applications, and historical financial records. Also, look into CRM systems, call center logs, and online banking platforms for customer interaction data.

4. **Collaborate with IT Department:** Work closely with the IT department to understand the bank's data infrastructure. They can assist in accessing data from various systems and guide you on data security protocols.

5. **Review Regulatory Constraints:** Be mindful of regulatory constraints related to data usage, especially around customer privacy and data protection laws like GDPR or CCPA. This is crucial in banking due to the sensitive nature of financial data.

6. **Use Publicly Available Data:** Augment internal data with publicly available datasets, such as economic indicators, stock market data, or public financial reports.

7. **Explore Data Aggregators and Third-party Providers:** Consider data from third-party providers or aggregators that offer banking and financial datasets for additional insights or benchmarking.

8. **Leverage Synthetic Data:** If accessing real data is difficult, use synthetic data generation techniques to create a proxy dataset resembling real banking data. *Refer to the Appendix on Synthetic Data Creation.*

9. **Utilize Data Warehouses and Data Lakes:** If available, use the bank's data warehouse or data lake, which often contain consolidated data from various sources.

10. **Data Mining Techniques:** Use data mining to extract information from large datasets, including text mining in customer emails, analyzing transaction

patterns, or conducting sentiment analysis on customer feedback.

11. Focus on Data Quality: Ensure high data quality, with data cleaning and preprocessing being essential steps. *See the Appendix on Data Quality Scores.*

12. Adhere to Ethical Standards: Follow ethical guidelines in data handling, especially with customer information. Maintaining transparency and customer trust is paramount.

13. Seek Legal and Compliance Advice: Consult legal and compliance teams before using sensitive or personal data to ensure compliance with all regulations.

14. Experiment with Pilot Projects: Initiate pilot projects using a small data subset to showcase the potential value of ML applications and gain access to more comprehensive data sets.

Step Two: Data Preprocessing Data preprocessing is a vital step in the machine learning pipeline, transforming raw data into a format suitable for ML models. Key steps include:

1. **Data Integration:** Combining data from different sources, which may involve merging datasets, aligning columns, and resolving inconsistencies in formats or units.

2. **Data Cleaning:** Correcting errors in the data, handling missing values, correcting typos or inaccuracies, and addressing outliers. *Refer to the Appendix on Data Cleaning.*
    - Missing values can be handled by imputation or deletion.
    - Outliers can be detected and either removed or corrected.

Step Three: Data Transformation

- **Normalization/Scaling:** Adjusting all variables to a similar scale, especially for models sensitive to input scale.

- **Applying Transformations:** Reducing skewness in data distribution using methods like logarithmic, square root, or power transformations.

Step Four: Data Reduction

- **Dimensionality Reduction:** Techniques like PCA or t-SNE to reduce the number of features.
- **Removing Irrelevant Features:** Eliminating features that don't contribute to the predictive power.

Step Five: Feature Engineering

- **Creating New Features:** Enhancing model performance by aggregating features, creating interaction features, or deriving new features.
- **Encoding Categorical Variables:** Using methods like one-hot encoding, label encoding, or binary encoding.

Step Six: Data Splitting

- **Training, Validation, and Test Sets:** Splitting data for model evaluation and to prevent overfitting, typically using a 70% (training), 15% (validation), 15% (testing) ratio, though this can vary.

Step Seven: Data Formatting

- **Formatting for Algorithm:** Ensuring data is in the correct format (arrays, tensors, etc.) for the chosen ML algorithm.

Step Eight: Handling Imbalanced Data

- **Balancing Classes:** Techniques like oversampling the minority class, undersampling the majority class, or using methods like SMOTE for classification problems with imbalanced classes.

Step Nine: Feature Selection

- **Selecting Relevant Features:** Using techniques such as mutual information, chi-square tests, or feature importance scores to choose the most effective features for the model.

Step Ten: Data Anonymization

- **Protecting Privacy:** Anonymizing sensitive data by removing personally identifiable information or employing techniques like k-anonymity to ensure privacy.

Data Preprocessing and the ML Process

Data preprocessing is a critical stage in machine learning that significantly influences the performance of models. It involves converting raw data into a format that is suitable for learning. Here's a closer look at the steps involved in the ML process post-data preprocessing:

1. Data Preprocessing:
    - **Raw Data Handling:** Cleaning data, handling missing values, normalizing data, and feature extraction.
    - **Importance:** Proper preprocessing ensures that the data fed into the model is accurate, relevant, and in a format conducive to learning.
2. Splitting Data:
    - **Training and Testing Sets:** The dataset is typically divided into training and testing sets. The training set is for training the model, while the testing set is used to evaluate its performance.
    - **Purpose:** This split helps in assessing the model's ability to generalize to new, unseen data, thus preventing overfitting.
3. Model Selection:
    - **Choosing the Right Model:** This depends on the problem type (classification, regression, etc.), the data's size and nature, and the algorithm's goal.
    - **Considerations:** The chosen model should align with the specific characteristics and requirements of the data and the problem.
4. Training the Model:

- **Learning from Data:** The model is trained on the training dataset, where it learns to make predictions or classifications by identifying patterns in the data.
- **Process:** This involves feeding the model with the training data and allowing it to adjust its parameters to improve prediction accuracy.

5. Model Evaluation:
- **Testing Performance:** The model is evaluated on a separate testing dataset to assess its performance.
- **Metrics:** Common evaluation metrics include accuracy, precision, recall, and the F1 score, which provide insights into the model's effectiveness.

6. Parameter Tuning and Optimization:
- **Fine-tuning the Model:** Based on evaluation results, the model might require adjustments, like tuning hyperparameters or modifying features, to enhance its performance.
- **Goal:** The aim is to optimize the model to achieve the best possible results on the given task.

7. Deployment:
- **Putting the Model to Use:** Once the model is fine-tuned and achieves satisfactory performance, it is deployed into a production environment.
- **Application:** In this stage, the model starts making predictions on new data, providing actionable insights or decisions in real-world scenarios.

Each of these steps is essential in developing a robust machine learning model. They ensure that the model is not only accurate in its predictions but also reliable and applicable in practical scenarios. The process from data preprocessing to model deployment involves a series of meticulous steps that are fundamental to the success of ML projects, especially in data-driven sectors like banking.

Final Step: Evaluating Your Machine Learning Model's Performance

Evaluating the accuracy and performance of a Machine Learning (ML) model is a critical final step in the ML process. The methods for evaluation depend on whether the model is for classification or regression, and on the specific requirements of the task. Here are common methods to measure the accuracy of ML models:

For Classification Models:

1. Accuracy Score:
   - Defined as the ratio of correctly predicted instances to the total instances.
   - Most effective when target classes are well balanced.
   - Formula:
     True Positives + True NegativesTotal Number of Sam plesTotal Number of SamplesTrue Positives + True N egatives
2. Confusion Matrix:
   - A table that visualizes the performance of the algorithm, showing true positives, false positives, true negatives, and false negatives.
   - Useful for understanding the types of errors made by the model.
3. Precision and Recall:
   - **Precision (Positive Predictive Value):** The ratio of true positive predictions to the total positive predictions, important when the cost of false positives is high.
   - **Recall (Sensitivity):** The ratio of true positive predictions to the total actual positives, vital when the cost of false negatives is high.
4. F1 Score:
   - The harmonic mean of precision and recall, balancing their trade-off.
   - Useful when considering both false positives and false negatives.

- Formula:
  2×Precision×RecallPrecision + Recall2×Precision + RecallPrecision×Recall
5. ROC Curve and AUC:
    - The ROC curve plots the true positive rate (Recall) against the false positive rate for various thresholds.
    - AUC measures the entire area underneath the ROC curve, with a higher AUC indicating a better-performing model.

For Regression Models:

1. Mean Absolute Error (MAE):
    - Measures the average magnitude of errors in predictions, without considering direction.
    - Formula: average(absolute(errors))average(absolute(errors))
2. Mean Squared Error (MSE):
    - Measures the average of the squares of the errors, penalizing larger errors more.
    - Formula: average(square(errors))average(square(errors))
3. Root Mean Squared Error (RMSE):
    - The square root of MSE, in the same units as the response variable, and sensitive to large errors.
4. R-squared (Coefficient of Determination):
    - Indicates the proportion of the variance in the dependent variable predictable from the independent variables.
    - Ranges from 0 to 1, with higher values indicating a better fit.
5. Adjusted R-squared:
    - Adjusts R-squared based on the number of predictors in the model, useful for comparing models with different numbers of independent variables.

Each of these evaluation methods provides different insights into the performance of an ML model, allowing practitioners to assess its effectiveness and suitability for the intended application. Accurate model evaluation is key to ensuring that the model performs reliably and effectively in real-world scenarios.

General Considerations in Evaluating Machine Learning Models

When evaluating Machine Learning (ML) models, it's important to employ comprehensive strategies to ensure accurate and reliable outcomes. Some general considerations include:

1. Cross-Validation:
    *   **Purpose:** To prevent overfitting and ensure that the model generalizes well to new data.
    *   **Method:** A common technique is K-fold cross-validation, where the dataset is divided into K subsets. The model is trained on K-1 subsets and tested on the remaining subset. This process is repeated K times, each time with a different subset as the test set.
2. Domain-Specific Evaluation Metrics:
    *   **Relevance:** In certain industries, such as finance, domain-specific metrics like Return on Investment (ROI) or Alpha may be more relevant than generic ML metrics.
    *   **Application:** These metrics can provide insights tailored to the specific goals and requirements of the domain.
3. Model Interpretability:
    *   **Importance:** Understanding the reasoning behind a model's predictions is essential, especially in sensitive fields like healthcare or finance.
    *   **Benefits:** Interpretability enhances trust in the model and helps in identifying potential biases or errors in its decision-making process.
4. Error Analysis:

- **Process:** Reviewing instances where the model performs poorly to understand the underlying reasons.
- **Outcome:** This analysis can guide necessary modifications or improvements to the model.

Chapter 3: A Primer on Artificial Intelligence Technologies

This chapter will provide an introduction to the fundamental concepts and key technologies that form the basis of Artificial Intelligence (AI) and Machine Learning (ML). It's designed to offer a foundational understanding crucial for anyone working with these technologies in the banking sector. This primer aims to demystify AI and ML, making these technologies more accessible and comprehensible, particularly for professionals in the banking industry who are increasingly relying on AI and ML for a range of applications from risk management to customer service. By understanding the core principles and mechanisms of AI and ML, banking professionals can better leverage these technologies to enhance their operations, decision-making processes, and customer engagement strategies.

Key AI Technologies in Banking

The banking sector increasingly employs various Artificial Intelligence (AI) technologies to improve efficiency, enhance customer experience, and manage risks. Here are some key AI technologies currently making a significant impact in banking:

1. Neural Networks:
   - **Description:** Inspired by the human brain, neural networks consist of interconnected nodes or 'neurons' that process and learn from data. They are structured in layers and learn complex patterns through extensive training.
   - **Applications in Banking:** Commonly used in tasks like image and speech recognition, fraud detection, and customer behavior analysis.
2. Natural Language Processing (NLP):
   - **Function:** NLP enables machines to understand, interpret, and respond to human language. It combines computational linguistics with machine learning models.
   - **Banking Applications:** NLP is instrumental in powering chatbots, enhancing customer service, and

conducting sentiment analysis on customer feedback.

3. Deep Learning:
   - **Overview:** As a subset of machine learning, deep learning uses multi-layered neural networks to analyze data. It is particularly adept at handling unstructured data such as images, text, and sound.
   - **Role in Banking:** Useful for identifying complex patterns and insights in large datasets, such as detecting fraudulent activities or analyzing customer interactions.

4. Reinforcement Learning:
   - **Mechanism:** This ML approach involves algorithms learning optimal actions through trial and error to achieve a specific goal.
   - **Banking Implementation:** Applied in scenarios requiring decision-making under uncertainty, like investment strategies or optimizing operational processes.

5. Predictive Analytics:
   - **Purpose:** These ML techniques predict future events based on historical data.
   - **Use in Banking:** Essential for forecasting customer behavior, assessing credit risks, and identifying market trends.

The growth in the field of ML has led to the development of numerous platforms and tools that aid in the creation and implementation of ML models. These advancements are not just technological but also represent a shift in how banks approach problem-solving and decision-making, with a growing reliance on data-driven insights.

As AI technologies continue to evolve, their applications in banking are likely to expand, offering more sophisticated and nuanced solutions to traditional banking challenges. These technologies are transforming the banking landscape, making operations more efficient, customer-centric, and adaptive to changing market dynamics.

Machine Learning Tools and Platforms: Open Source Options

Among open-source tools for machine learning and data science, Jupyter Notebook holds a prominent place. Here's an overview of its features, role, and comparison with full-fledged ML platforms:

Jupyter Notebook:

1. Description:
   - Jupyter Notebook is an open-source web application that allows the creation and sharing of documents containing live code, equations, visualizations, and narrative text.
   - Commonly used for data cleaning, transformation, numerical simulation, statistical modeling, data visualization, and preliminary stages of machine learning.
2. Key Features:
   - Supports over 40 programming languages, including Python, R, Julia, and Scala.
   - Notebooks can contain rich media, interactive graphs, and widgets.
   - Facilitates a literate programming approach, making it ideal for education, data analysis, and reporting.
3. Role in ML Workflows:
   - Widely used for exploratory data analysis, prototype model development, and visualization.
   - Great for initial stages of ML model development like data exploration, feature engineering, and preliminary model training.

Comparison with Full-Fledged ML Platforms:

- While Jupyter Notebook is a powerful tool for various aspects of ML and data science projects, it doesn't provide the comprehensive functionalities of full-scale ML platforms like TensorFlow or AWS SageMaker.
- These advanced platforms offer capabilities beyond development, including model training, evaluation,

deployment, monitoring, data storage, version control, and model hosting services, essential for complete ML project development.

Jupyter in the Ecosystem:

- Jupyter Notebooks are often integrated into ML platforms as an Interactive Development Environment (IDE) for model development and experimentation.
- In the broader data science and ML ecosystem, Jupyter plays a vital role as an interactive development tool but is typically used in conjunction with other tools and platforms throughout the ML project lifecycle.

In summary, Jupyter Notebook is an invaluable tool in the ML and data science toolkit, particularly for exploratory work, visualization, and early-stage model development. However, it is generally part of a larger suite of tools and platforms used in the full lifecycle of ML projects, excelling in facilitating exploration and initial development phases.

Overview of "Jupyter-like" Tools in Data Science and Machine Learning

Several tools offer functionalities similar to Jupyter Notebooks, providing environments conducive to interactive computing, data analysis, and machine learning. These tools often combine code execution with rich text and visualization capabilities. Some notable alternatives and similar tools include:

1. Apache Zeppelin:
   - A web-based notebook that facilitates interactive data analytics.
   - Known for its integration with Apache Spark and Hadoop ecosystems.
   - Supports SQL, Scala, Python, R, and more.
2. Google Colab (Colaboratory):
   - A free cloud-based Jupyter notebook environment.

- Offers free access to computing resources, including GPUs and TPUs.
- Popular for ML and data analysis projects.

3. RStudio and R Markdown:
   - RStudio is an Integrated Development Environment (IDE) for R.
   - R Markdown combines R code with Markdown annotations, allowing documents to be compiled into various formats like HTML, PDF, and Word.
   - Supports interactive content and is commonly used for data analysis and reporting.

4. Observable:
   - A reactive notebook platform focused on data visualization.
   - Allows users to create, collaborate, and share using JavaScript.
   - Extensively used for interactive data stories and visualizations.

5. Databricks Notebooks:
   - Offers a collaborative environment with a notebook-like interface.
   - Supports Python, R, Scala, SQL, and integrates with Apache Spark for big data processing.

6. Kaggle Kernels:
   - A cloud-based Jupyter notebook environment provided by Kaggle.
   - Supports Python and R, offering free access to computational resources like GPUs.
   - Widely used for Kaggle competitions and collaborative data science projects.

7. Azure Notebooks:
   - A free, cloud-based Jupyter notebook service from Microsoft.
   - Supports Python, R, and F# with integration with Azure services.
   - Facilitates sharing and collaboration.

8. SageMathCell:

- A web-based computational environment based on SageMath.
- Designed for embedding Sage computations into web pages and documents.

9. nteract:
- A desktop application for working with Jupyter notebooks as a standalone, native application.
- Supports interactive data visualization and various kernels.

10. JupyterLab:
- An advanced web-based user interface for Jupyter.
- Offers a flexible and powerful environment for working with Jupyter notebooks and other documents.

These tools have become increasingly popular in the data science and academic communities for their ability to facilitate interactive data exploration, visualization, and collaboration. Each tool offers unique features and integrations, making them suited for different aspects of data science and ML projects.

Overview of Machine Learning (ML) Platforms

A Machine Learning (ML) platform is an integrated suite of tools and technologies that streamline the development, training, evaluation, and deployment of ML models. These platforms are designed to support various stages of the ML workflow and cater to a wide range of needs in the data science and machine learning fields. Key characteristics and components of an ML platform include:

1. Data Handling and Preprocessing:
- Tools for collecting, processing, and managing large datasets.
- Includes capabilities for data cleaning, normalization, transformation, and feature extraction.

2. Model Development Environment:
- A user-friendly interface for developing ML models.

- Support for various ML libraries and frameworks like TensorFlow, PyTorch, or Scikit-Learn.
3. Algorithm Selection and Training:
    - A range of built-in algorithms for different ML tasks (classification, regression, clustering, etc.).
    - Ability to train models using these algorithms.
4. Model Evaluation and Tuning:
    - Tools for assessing model performance using various metrics and techniques.
    - Features for tuning hyperparameters to improve model accuracy and efficiency.
5. Scalability and Performance Optimization:
    - Capability to handle large-scale data and complex models.
    - Often includes parallel processing, distributed computing, and optimization for high-performance hardware.
6. Integration and Automation:
    - Features for integration with other software tools and systems.
    - Automation of the ML workflow for more efficient development.
7. Model Deployment and Monitoring:
    - Tools for deploying trained models into production environments.
    - Monitoring and managing model performance over time.
8. Collaboration and Version Control:
    - Support for collaborative model development and version control.
9. Security and Compliance:
    - Ensuring data security, privacy, and adherence to regulatory standards.
10. Customization and Extensibility:
    - Ability to customize the platform and extend its capabilities for specific project needs or integration with existing infrastructure.

ML platforms can be cloud-based, offering extensive resources and scalability, or on-premises installations that provide more control and security. They aim to make the ML process more accessible and efficient for both seasoned data scientists and newcomers to the field. By offering a comprehensive suite of tools, these platforms significantly reduce the complexity and time involved in developing and deploying machine learning models.

Overview of Prominent Machine Learning Platforms and Libraries
The landscape of Machine Learning (ML) platforms and libraries is diverse, each offering unique features and capabilities. Here's a snapshot of some of the most prominent ones:

1. TensorFlow:
   - Developed by Google, this open-source library is used for numerical computation and ML.
   - Known for its deep learning capabilities, TensorFlow offers flexible tools for building and deploying ML models.
2. PyTorch:
   - Created by Facebook's AI Research lab, PyTorch is an open-source ML library.
   - It stands out for its ease of use, flexibility, and dynamic computational graph, making it a favorite for deep learning research and development.
3. Scikit-Learn:
   - A Python-based library, Scikit-Learn is popular for traditional ML algorithms.
   - Offers tools for classification, regression, clustering, and dimensionality reduction, and is praised for its simplicity and ease of use.
4. Keras:
   - Now integrated with TensorFlow, Keras is an open-source neural network library in Python.

- Designed for fast experimentation with deep neural networks, it is known for its user-friendliness and modularity.
5. Microsoft Azure Machine Learning:
    - Azure ML is a cloud-based platform from Microsoft offering tools for ML model building, training, and deployment.
    - It supports various ML frameworks and provides a collaborative environment for ML projects.
6. Amazon SageMaker:
    - A fully managed service from AWS, SageMaker enables quick building, training, and deployment of ML models.
    - Offers capabilities including a Jupyter notebook instance for model development.
7. Google Cloud AI Platform:
    - A suite of services from Google Cloud for building ML models.
    - Includes tools for data preparation, job training, and model prediction, integrated with Google Cloud services.
8. IBM Watson:
    - Provides a suite of AI and ML services for building and deploying AI models and applications.
    - Known for its advanced NLP capabilities and application in various business contexts.
9. RapidMiner:
    - A data science platform that offers an integrated environment for data preparation, ML, deep learning, text mining, and predictive analytics.
    - Known for its visual workflow designer and user-friendly interface.
10. H2O:
    - An open-source, distributed in-memory ML platform, H2O is known for its scalability.
    - Supports widely used statistical and ML algorithms, and is notable for its speed and performance.

The choice of a specific platform or library often depends on project requirements, existing infrastructure, and the team's expertise. Each platform has its strengths, catering to different aspects of the ML workflow, from data preprocessing to model deployment.
Understanding the unique features and capabilities of these platforms can help in selecting the most appropriate tool for a given ML project.

Additional Resources in Machine Learning

In addition to the comprehensive ML platforms and libraries, there are other resources that provide unique contributions to the field of machine learning, especially for specific tasks like competitions and natural language processing.

1. Kaggle:
   - **Description:** Best known for hosting machine learning competitions, Kaggle offers a collaborative and competitive environment for data scientists and ML practitioners.
   - **Features:** Provides access to a rich repository of datasets and Kaggle Kernels (now Kaggle Code), a cloud-based Jupyter notebook environment.
   - **Usage:** Ideal for learning, experimentation, and engaging with a community of ML professionals. Users can work on real-world data problems, share solutions, and learn from others.
   - **Limitations:** While valuable for learning and experimentation, Kaggle is less focused on the complete ML development lifecycle, particularly in deploying models in production environments.
   - **Advantages:** Allows running models that have been curated and ranked, and offers the option to upload your data or download the code and data for local use.
2. Hugging Face:
   - **Specialization:** Known for its significant contributions to Natural Language Processing (NLP).

- **Offerings:** Hosts a vast collection of pre-trained models, particularly transformer models like BERT and GPT, accessible via its library.
- **Functionality:** Provides ready-to-use NLP models and a collaborative platform for building and sharing models.
- **Focus:** Hugging Face is specialized in the NLP domain and doesn't offer the broader range of functionalities of full-scale ML platforms.

Both Kaggle and Hugging Face serve as valuable resources in the ML community, offering unique advantages for specific needs. Kaggle is a go-to for those looking to engage in competitions, access diverse datasets, and learn from a community, whereas Hugging Face is ideal for those focused on NLP, offering state-of-the-art pre-trained models and a collaborative environment for NLP model development. These platforms complement the more comprehensive ML tools and platforms by providing specialized functionalities and community-driven learning opportunities.

Chapter 4: Uncovering Opportunities for AI in Regional Banks

This chapter outlines various strategies to identify opportunities for the application of Artificial Intelligence (AI) in regional banks, focusing on operational excellence and cost efficiency. These strategies aim to pinpoint pain points, especially manual tasks and error-prone areas, where AI automation can be effectively applied.

1. Process Mapping and Analysis:
   - Conduct a comprehensive operational review, documenting each process step, resources, inputs, outputs, and responsible personnel.
   - Focus on identifying inefficiencies or bottlenecks that hinder smooth operations.

2. Customer Feedback and Surveys:
   - Regularly collect and analyze customer feedback for insights on common complaints and improvement areas.
   - Utilize survey data to pinpoint challenges in account management, customer service, and digital banking experiences.

3. Employee Feedback and Interviews:
   - Engage with employees at all levels to understand their challenges and ideas for improvement.
   - Explore opinions on repetitive tasks that could be automated.

4. Data Analysis:
   - Analyze transaction records and customer service logs to identify recurring issues or inefficiencies.
   - Employ data analytics and AI tools for trend analysis that highlight operational pain points.

5. Regulatory and Compliance Assessment:
   - Evaluate compliance processes, identifying areas where automation can enhance accuracy and timeliness.

6. Technology Assessment:

- Review current technology infrastructure for inefficiencies caused by outdated or un-integrated systems.
- Identify system upgrades and integration opportunities to streamline operations.

7. Benchmarking and Industry Research:
   - Conduct comparative analysis against industry standards and competitors to identify improvement areas through automation.
8. Supplier and Vendor Relationships:
   - Evaluate third-party relationships for automation opportunities in communication, payment processing, and supply chain management.
9. Customer Journey Mapping:
   - Develop comprehensive customer journey maps to identify critical touchpoints for automation to improve service quality and reduce wait times.
10. Fraud Detection and Risk Analysis:
    - Use historical data to detect fraud patterns and identify areas for AI-powered security improvements.
11. Operational Efficiency Audits:
    - Conduct regular audits to pinpoint excessive operational costs and identify automation opportunities.
12. Customer Attrition Analysis:
    - Analyze customer attrition data to understand the reasons behind customer departures and address these through targeted automation.
13. Digital Channel Analytics:
    - Assess digital interactions to determine where AI-enhanced tools can improve user experiences.
14. Compliance Monitoring:
    - Implement AI tools for continuous transaction monitoring to ensure adherence to regulations and automate suspicious activity reporting.
15. Predictive Maintenance:

- Utilize IoT sensors and AI for predictive maintenance of physical assets like ATMs to reduce downtime and maintenance costs.

By employing these strategies, regional banks can identify key areas where AI can bring significant improvements, enhancing operational efficiency, customer satisfaction, and overall competitiveness in the financial sector.

Monetizing Data in Regional Banks

Regional banks, with their extensive and diverse data repositories, are in a prime position to monetize this data effectively. By employing various strategies, they can unlock significant market value, leading to new revenue streams while enhancing their services. Here are some ways banks can capitalize on their data:

1. Customer Analytics Services:
   - Offer insights into consumer behavior and market trends by anonymizing and aggregating customer data.
   - In demand by retail, e-commerce, and marketing industries.
2. Credit Scoring and Risk Assessment Tools:
   - Develop sophisticated credit scoring models and risk assessment tools for sale to other financial institutions and credit reporting agencies.
3. Fraud Detection and Prevention Solutions:
   - Leverage expertise in transaction analysis to create fraud detection solutions for financial institutions and e-commerce platforms.
4. Data-as-a-Service (DaaS):
   - Provide access to specific datasets, like transaction data and economic indicators, on a subscription or volume-based pricing model.
5. Financial Market Insights:
   - Create research reports and insights for investors and fund managers using bank data.

6. Personal Finance Applications:
   - Develop apps or tools for budgeting and financial management, monetizing through subscriptions or premium features.
7. APIs and Integrations:
   - Create APIs for third-party developers, offering services like account aggregation or payment processing.
8. Tailored Investment Services:
   - Use customer data to provide personalized investment recommendations, monetizing through asset management fees.
9. Data Licensing:
   - License datasets to research firms or government agencies, including data on economic indicators or consumer behaviors.
10. Partnerships with Fintech Startups:
    - Collaborate with fintech startups to develop innovative financial products, benefiting from revenue-sharing models.
11. Cross-Sell and Upsell Opportunities:
    - Utilize data analytics to identify cross-selling and upselling opportunities within the existing customer base.
12. Customer Insights for Retailers:
    - Partner with retailers to provide customer behavior insights, helping them optimize marketing strategies and product offerings.
13. Economic Forecasting Services:
    - Develop forecasting models to provide insights for businesses, policymakers, and investors.

Through these strategies, regional banks can transform their data into a valuable asset, generating new revenue while enhancing their service offerings. This approach not only contributes to the bank's financial growth but also positions them as innovative leaders in utilizing data for diverse applications beyond traditional banking services.

Chapter 5: Building an AI-Ready Infrastructure

After selecting an AI use-case (refer to the appendix for a comprehensive list), the next critical step is to set up an effective data infrastructure. This involves assessing, categorizing, and ensuring the quality of your data.

Building an AI-Ready Infrastructure: Data Management Steps

Step 1: Data Assessment and Inventory

1. Data Categorization:
   - **Categorize Data Sets:** Begin by categorizing your data sets based on specific Machine Learning (ML) use cases. This involves associating each data set with its intended AI or ML application, such as customer segmentation, fraud detection, or demand forecasting.
   - **Use Case Alignment:** Ensure that each data set is precisely aligned with the ML use case it is intended for. This alignment is crucial for maintaining clarity and relevance during the data infrastructure setup.

2. Data Quality Assessment Scoring:
   - **Data Quality Score:** Assign a Data Quality Score to each data set. This score evaluates the data's cleanliness and reliability for its intended use case, considering factors like completeness, accuracy, consistency, and timeliness.
   - **Data Set Quality Score:** Calculate a Data Set Quality Score for each ML use case by aggregating the Data Quality Scores of the associated data sets. This score provides an overall assessment of the data quality available for a specific ML project. It helps determine the suitability of the data for different types of ML algorithms, such as clustering, regression, etc.
   - **Comparative Analysis:** A practical approach is to compare your data sets with a benchmark data frame from a platform like Kaggle, used for a similar

application. This comparison can help identify gaps and areas for improvement in your data.

-

Data Audit and Documentation

1. Data Audit:
   - Conduct thorough audits of each data set to identify issues like missing values, outliers, and inconsistencies.
   - Document all findings to provide a clear picture of the data quality and areas that need attention.
2. Data Dictionary:
   - Create a comprehensive data dictionary detailing the metadata, schema, and attributes of each data set.
   - Include definitions, data types, and any transformations that have been applied to the data.

Data Governance

1. Data Governance Policies:
   - Establish robust data governance policies to maintain data quality and integrity.
   - Include protocols for data access controls, versioning, and auditing to ensure consistent data management.
2. Data Ownership:
   - Define clear data ownership responsibilities within the organization.
   - This step is crucial for ensuring accountability for data quality and adherence to compliance standards.

Step 2: Data Collection and Integration

1. Data Collection:
   - Implement effective data collection mechanisms for each categorized data set.
   - Ensure consistency in data collection and alignment with governance policies.

2. Data Integration:
   - Develop data integration pipelines to centralize and consolidate data from diverse sources.
   - These pipelines should cater to different use cases and ensure seamless data integration.

Step 3: Data Cleaning and Preparation

1. Data Cleaning:
   - Execute a comprehensive data cleaning process, addressing issues identified during the data audit.
   - Leverage automated tools and scripts for efficiency and consistency.
2. Data Transformation:
   - Transform and structure data to suit ML modeling requirements.
   - Apply necessary feature engineering and data normalization techniques specific to each ML use case.

Step 4: Data Storage and Management

1. Data Storage:
   - Choose appropriate data storage solutions (like data lakes or data warehouses) based on data volume and type.
   - Ensure the storage solution aligns with the data's categorization and quality.
2. Data Catalog:
   - Implement a data catalog to organize and index data sets, based on ML use cases and Data Set Quality Scores.

Guide to Building a Scalable Computing Infrastructure in Regional Banks

Establishing a scalable computing infrastructure is crucial for regional banks to handle increasing workloads, maintain performance, and facilitate future growth. Here is a structured approach to developing such an infrastructure:

Step 1: Assess Current Infrastructure

1. Infrastructure Audit:
   - Conduct a comprehensive audit of the existing computing infrastructure, including hardware, software, and network components.
   - This step is critical to understand the current state and capabilities of the infrastructure.
2. Performance Analysis:
   - Analyze the performance and capacity utilization of the current setup.
   - Identify any bottlenecks or areas that require upgrades or improvements to meet future demands.

Step 2: Define Infrastructure Requirements

1. Gather Requirements:
   - Collaborate with key stakeholders, such as IT staff, management, and end-users, to define the infrastructure requirements.
   - Consider factors like anticipated workload growth, regulatory compliance needs, and budget constraints.
2. Scalability Goals:
   - Clearly outline scalability goals, specifying metrics for performance, capacity, and scalability.
   - These goals will guide the selection of infrastructure components and technologies.

Step 3: Select Scalable Components

1. Cloud vs. On-Premises:
   - Evaluate the benefits and limitations of cloud-based versus on-premises solutions.

- Consider a hybrid approach, which combines the flexibility of the cloud with the control of on-premises infrastructure.
2. Scalable Servers:
   - Opt for servers designed for scalability, like rack-mounted or blade servers.
   - Prioritize key features such as processing power, memory, and storage capacity.
3. Virtualization:
   - Implement server virtualization technologies, such as VMware or Hyper-V.
   - Virtualization enhances resource utilization, workload management, and overall efficiency.

Step 4: Networking Infrastructure

1. High-Performance Network:
   - Upgrade to a network infrastructure capable of handling increased traffic without bottlenecks.
   - Invest in high-performance networking hardware, including switches, routers, and firewalls.
2. Redundancy:
   - Incorporate redundancy in the network to minimize potential downtime.
   - Utilize technologies like load balancing and failover mechanisms to ensure network availability and resilience.

Step 5: Storage Solutions

1. Storage Scalability:
   - Opt for scalable storage solutions like Network-Attached Storage (NAS) or Storage Area Networks (SANs) to manage increasing data volumes.
   - These solutions should adapt to growing data requirements without significant infrastructure overhauls.

2. Data Tiering:
   - Implement a data tiering strategy, storing frequently accessed data on high-performance storage systems, while allocating less frequently accessed data to lower-cost storage options.
   - This approach optimizes storage costs and performance efficiency.

Step 6: Cloud Integration

1. Cloud Services:
   - Utilize cloud services for enhanced scalability, particularly for burstable workloads, data backups, and disaster recovery processes.
   - Cloud services offer flexibility and cost-efficiency, especially for variable data demands.
2. Hybrid Cloud:
   - A hybrid cloud strategy, combining on-premises infrastructure with cloud resources, offers the best of both worlds.
   - Ensure seamless integration and interoperability between on-premises and cloud environments for smooth operations.

Step 7: Security and Compliance

1. Data Security:
   - Implement comprehensive security measures, including encryption, access controls, and regular security audits, to protect sensitive financial data.
   - Continuously update and strengthen security protocols to combat evolving cyber threats.
2. Compliance:
   - Ensure that the infrastructure adheres to banking and financial industry regulations, such as GLBA, PCI DSS, and regional standards.
   - Regular compliance checks and updates are vital to avoid legal and financial repercussions.

Step 8: Monitoring and Management

1. Infrastructure Monitoring:
   - Deploy advanced monitoring tools for real-time tracking of infrastructure performance, health, and security.
   - Proactive monitoring aids in early detection and resolution of potential issues.
2. Automation:
   - Utilize automation tools and scripts for efficient management of tasks like provisioning, scaling, and maintenance.
   - Automation reduces manual labor, minimizes errors, and increases operational efficiency.

Step 9: Disaster Recovery and Business Continuity

1. Backup and Recovery:
   - Establish a strong backup and recovery framework to safeguard critical data against loss or corruption.
   - Regular testing of recovery procedures ensures preparedness for data loss scenarios.
2. Business Continuity Planning:
   - Develop a thorough business continuity plan encompassing disaster recovery scenarios.
   - Such planning is essential for minimizing downtime and maintaining operational continuity in case of unforeseen events.

Step 10: Scalability Testing

1. Load Testing:
   - Conduct load testing to verify the infrastructure's capacity to handle projected workloads.
   - Identify and address performance bottlenecks to ensure smooth functioning under peak loads.
2. Scalability Testing:

- Perform scalability testing to confirm that the infrastructure can efficiently scale up or down according to varying demand levels.
- This testing is crucial for validating the infrastructure's readiness to accommodate future growth and changes in demand.

Step 11: Documentation and Training

1. Documentation:
   - Maintain comprehensive documentation of the computing infrastructure. This should include configurations, operational procedures, and troubleshooting guides.
   - Accurate documentation is vital for effective management and quick resolution of any issues that may arise.
2. Staff Training:
   - Conduct training programs for IT staff who will manage and maintain the infrastructure.
   - Training should cover essential aspects of scalability, performance optimization, and security, ensuring the team is proficient in managing a scalable infrastructure.

Step 12: Regular Evaluation and Optimization

1. Performance Monitoring:
   - Implement continuous monitoring of infrastructure performance and scalability metrics.
   - Regular monitoring allows for timely identification and optimization of any performance issues.
2. Cost Optimization:
   - Periodically review infrastructure costs and explore opportunities for cost optimization, such as through resource consolidation or rightsizing cloud resources.

- Effective cost management is crucial for maximizing the value of the infrastructure investments.

Additional Considerations

- Cloud vs. On-Premises:
  - Decide between cloud-based and on-premises solutions based on factors like scalability, cost, and specific resource requirements for ML workloads.
  - The choice will depend on the bank's operational model, regulatory requirements, and specific use cases.
- High-Performance Computing:
  - Set up high-performance computing clusters or GPUs, particularly for AI use cases that require significant computational power.
  - Such setups are essential for efficiently handling complex AI computations, including deep learning and large-scale data processing.

Conclusion

By following these comprehensive steps, regional banks can establish a structured and scalable computing infrastructure that caters to their current requirements and positions them well for future growth. The process of categorizing data sets, assessing and improving data quality, and aligning infrastructure with ML use cases is critical for a successful AI implementation. The inclusion of Data Quality Scores and Data Set Quality Scores aids in quantifying and enhancing data quality in line with the relevance of each use case. This approach not only ensures the scalability and performance of the infrastructure but also underpins the bank's ability to leverage AI and ML for advanced analytical capabilities, thereby providing exceptional customer service and maintaining a competitive edge in the financial industry.

Top of Form

Chapter 6: Self-Service Data, it's required

Self-service data access is a crucial enabler for Artificial Intelligence (AI) and Machine Learning (ML) initiatives. It allows data scientists, analysts, and other users to independently access and utilize data without relying on IT specialists or data stewards. This autonomy fosters a more agile, efficient, and innovative approach to AI and ML projects.

Benefits of Self-Service Data Access for AI and ML:

1. Reduced Time to Insights:
   - Self-service data access significantly accelerates the process of extracting insights and developing models by allowing users to quickly find and access the necessary data.
   - This swift access to data is instrumental in reducing the time between data acquisition and actionable insights.
2. Increased Productivity:
   - By eliminating reliance on IT teams for data retrieval, self-service data access enables data scientists and analysts to focus more on their primary tasks of analysis, modeling, and innovation.
   - This independence streamlines the workflow and enhances overall productivity.
3. Improved Data Utilization:
   - Self-service access promotes a broader exploration and utilization of data within the organization.
   - This expanded use of data cultivates a more data-driven culture, leading to enhanced decision-making processes.
4. Empowered Users:
   - Self-service access empowers users to be more autonomous and self-reliant in their data needs.
   - It fosters a sense of ownership and responsibility towards data quality and usage among the users.
5. Scalable Data Access:

- Self-service data platforms can be scaled to accommodate an increasing number of users and expanding data sources.
- This scalability is crucial for organizations dealing with growing data volumes and complexity.

Achieving Self-Service Data Access

Implementing self-service data access is pivotal for maximizing the efficiency and effectiveness of AI and ML initiatives. Here are key strategies to achieve this:

1. Data Catalog and Metadata Management:
   - Establish a centralized data catalog that provides detailed metadata about data assets. This includes descriptions, lineage, and access permissions.
   - A comprehensive data catalog is essential for users to understand what data is available, its source, and how it can be used.
2. Data Discovery and Search:
   - Implement intuitive search capabilities within the data catalog.
   - Allow users to easily discover relevant data based on criteria such as content, source, or usage patterns.
3. Data Access Controls and Governance:
   - Implement robust data access controls that are aligned with user roles and permissions.
   - Ensure that these controls facilitate data security and compliance, while also providing authorized access to users.
4. Data Access Tools and APIs:
   - Provide a range of data access tools and APIs that enable users to retrieve, manipulate, and analyze data directly.
   - These tools should be user-friendly and require minimal technical expertise, allowing users to work independently.

5. User Education and Training:
    - Offer comprehensive training and support to help users effectively navigate the data catalog, understand data policies, and utilize data access tools.
    - Regular training ensures users are up-to-date with the latest tools and best practices in data usage.
6. Continuous Monitoring and Improvement:
    - Regularly monitor data access patterns, gather user feedback, and assess system performance.
    - Use these insights to continuously refine and improve the self-service data access experience, addressing any issues and adapting to changing needs.

Why a Data Catalog is Essential in AI and ML

In the realm of AI and ML, a well-constructed data catalog is indispensable. It serves as a centralized platform that not only facilitates comprehensive data discovery and understanding but also ensures granular data access control, user-friendly data tools, and adaptability to the ever-evolving data landscape. This, in turn, significantly empowers AI and ML practitioners to work more efficiently, innovate rapidly, and make informed, data-driven decisions. Here are the key reasons why a data catalog is a must-have:

1. Data Discovery and Exploration:
    - Provides a searchable interface for easy discovery of relevant data assets.
    - Simplifies the process of identifying and exploring data sources for AI and ML projects.
2. Data Understanding and Context:
    - Stores detailed metadata about data assets, including descriptions, lineage, and usage patterns.
    - Offers vital contextual information that aids in understanding data origins, quality, and potential biases.

3. Data Quality Assessment:
   - Integrates with data quality tools for assessing data completeness, accuracy, and consistency.
   - Enables early identification and rectification of data quality issues, crucial for reliable model training.
4. Data Governance and Compliance:
   - Facilitates data governance and compliance by tracking data access, usage, and changes.
   - Ensures adherence to data policies, regulatory requirements, and data privacy standards.
5. Collaboration and Communication:
   - Acts as a shared platform for collaboration among data users.
   - Encourages sharing of data documentation, annotations, and insights.
6. Model Development and Deployment:
   - Streamlines model development by providing a repository for data management and versioning.
   - Enhances reproducibility and tracks model performance over time.
7. Accelerated AI and ML Projects:
   - Reduces the time and effort required for data-related aspects of AI and ML projects.
   - Allows practitioners to concentrate on critical tasks like model development and evaluation.
8. Improved Model Performance and Reliability:
   - Improves model performance by providing access to high-quality, relevant data.
   - Facilitates collaboration, contributing to more reliable and generalizable models.
9. Reduced Data Duplication and Waste:
   - Helps identify and eliminate data duplication, optimizing storage costs.
   - Ensures the use of the most current and accurate data.
10. Enhanced Data Literacy and Awareness:
    - Promotes data literacy within the organization.

- Leads to improved data management practices and a data-driven organizational culture.

A data catalog is thus an integral component in the infrastructure supporting AI and ML, enhancing data accessibility, quality, governance, and collaboration, all of which are critical for the success of AI and ML initiatives.

Introducing the Data Quality Score

The Data Quality Score is a crucial metric in managing and leveraging data effectively, especially in contexts where data-driven decision-making, like AI and ML, is paramount. The Unified Data Quality Score (UDQS) and Data Set Quality Score (DSQS) are key tools in this regard. They help quantify the quality of structured data across several dimensions, ensuring that the data used in various projects is of high quality and reliability.

Key Aspects of the Data Quality Score:

1. Unified Data Quality Score (UDQS):
    - This score assesses the overall quality of an individual data set.
    - It evaluates dimensions such as completeness, consistency, accuracy, and timeliness of the data.
    - UDQS is crucial for understanding the reliability and usability of a specific data set.
2. Data Set Quality Score (DSQS):
    - DSQS aggregates the UDQS of multiple data sets to provide an overall quality score for a collection of data related to a specific project or use case.
    - It helps in assessing the collective quality of data that will be used in a particular analysis or model.

Importance of Data Quality Scores:

- Identifying and Prioritizing Data Quality Issues:
    - These scores help in pinpointing specific areas where data quality falls short, allowing for targeted improvements.

- Prioritizing data quality issues based on their impact on analysis or decision-making becomes more manageable.
- Monitoring Data Quality Over Time:
    - Regular calculation of UDQS and DSQS offers a way to monitor the quality of data over time.
    - This ongoing assessment is vital for maintaining high data standards in dynamic environments where data constantly evolves.
- Selecting the Best Data for Projects:
    - By providing a quantifiable measure of data quality, these scores aid in selecting the most suitable data sets for specific AI and ML projects.
    - High-quality data is a prerequisite for accurate and reliable outcomes in data-driven projects.

Conclusion:

The Data Quality Score, encompassing both UDQS and DSQS, plays a pivotal role in ensuring that the data used in AI and ML projects is of high quality. By quantitatively assessing data across various quality dimensions, these scores provide a comprehensive view of data reliability and suitability, which is essential for successful data-driven initiatives. In an era where data is a key strategic asset, effective data quality management using UDQS and DSQS becomes indispensable.

Chapter 7: Challenges and Considerations in Implementing AI and ML in Regional Banks

Implementing AI and ML in regional banks comes with its unique set of challenges and considerations. This chapter delves into critical areas such as data privacy and security, ethical implications and bias, as well as technical and organizational hurdles.

Data Privacy and Security:

1. Privacy Concerns:
   - With AI and ML relying extensively on data, safeguarding customer information is paramount.
   - Banks must comply with complex data privacy regulations, like the GDPR in Europe and the CCPA in California, among others.
   - Balancing data utilization for AI with privacy requirements is a significant challenge.

2. Security Risks:
   - Incorporating AI into banking systems introduces new vectors for cyberattacks.
   - Security of AI systems is crucial, as breaches can lead to substantial data loss and severely damage customer trust.
   - Proactive and continuous security measures are needed to protect AI systems from evolving cyber threats.

3. Data Management:
   - Maintaining the integrity, confidentiality, and availability of data within AI systems is a complex task.
   - Banks need to establish strong data governance frameworks to effectively manage data risks.
   - This includes implementing policies and practices for data quality, access control, and compliance.

Ethical Considerations and Bias:
- AI systems can inadvertently perpetuate biases, leading to unfair or unethical outcomes, particularly in sensitive areas like credit scoring or fraud detection.
- Ensuring AI algorithms are transparent, explainable, and fair is essential.
- Regular auditing of AI systems for bias and implementing corrective measures is crucial to maintain ethical standards.

Technical and Organizational Challenges:
- Integration with Legacy Systems:
    - Many banks operate on legacy systems that may not seamlessly integrate with modern AI technologies.
    - Upgrading or adapting these systems to work with AI can be technically challenging and costly.
- Skill Gaps:
    - There is often a skills gap in the existing workforce regarding AI and ML technologies.
    - Investing in training and possibly hiring new talent is essential to bridge this gap.
- Cultural Resistance:
    - In some cases, there may be organizational resistance to adopting AI, stemming from concerns about job displacement or distrust in automated systems.
    - Addressing these concerns through education and demonstrating the value of AI in augmenting human capabilities is vital.
- Cost Considerations:
    - Implementing AI can require significant investment in technology, training, and process reengineering.
    - Banks need to assess the cost-benefit ratio and plan for long-term ROI.

Ethical Considerations and Bias in AI:
1. Algorithmic Bias:
    - AI algorithms may inadvertently reinforce biases present in the training data, potentially leading to

unfair or discriminatory outcomes, especially in sensitive areas like credit scoring.
- Continuous monitoring and adjusting of algorithms are essential to mitigate these biases.
2. Transparency and Accountability:
   - AI systems in banking need to be transparent, with clear accountability for decisions made by AI algorithms.
   - Banks must ensure that AI decision-making processes are understandable and explainable to stakeholders.
3. Ethical Use:
   - Ethical use of AI, respecting customer rights and societal norms, is paramount.
   - Developing and adhering to ethical frameworks and guidelines is crucial for responsible AI deployment.

Technical and Organizational Challenges:
1. Integration with Existing Systems:
   - Integrating AI and ML with legacy banking systems poses significant technical challenges.
   - Careful planning is required to ensure compatibility and efficient operation.
2. Skill Gap:
   - A skill gap often exists in the workforce regarding AI and ML.
   - Investing in training, and possibly recruiting specialized talent, is necessary for successful AI implementation.
3. Change Management:
   - Adopting AI and ML involves significant changes in processes and culture.
   - Effectively managing this change, addressing employee concerns, and securing buy-in is vital.
4. Maintaining Model Accuracy and Relevance:
   - AI and ML models need constant monitoring and updating to ensure ongoing accuracy and relevance.

Essential Technology Infrastructure:
1. Robust Data Management Systems:
   - Advanced data management systems are crucial for handling the diverse data types in banking.
   - These systems form the foundation of an efficient AI infrastructure.
2. Scalable Computing Resources:
   - AI and ML demand substantial computational power.
   - Investment in scalable computing resources, such as cloud computing or powerful in-house servers, is essential.
3. Secure Networking Capabilities:
   - Secure and reliable networking infrastructure is crucial for the safe transfer of sensitive banking data.
   - Ensuring data security during transmission is critical.
4. Advanced Analytics Tools:
   - Tools for data visualization, statistical analysis, and advanced analytics are essential for deriving insights from data, a key step in AI applications.
5. AI Software and Platforms:
   - Utilizing AI software and platforms tailored for banking applications can facilitate smoother implementation and integration.

Developing In-House AI Expertise vs. Outsourcing

Regional banks face a strategic decision in their AI and ML journey: whether to develop AI expertise in-house or to outsource it. Each approach has its unique benefits and considerations.

Benefits of In-House AI Development:

1. Customized Solutions:
   - In-house development allows banks to tailor AI solutions specifically to their unique needs and operational context.

- This can result in more effective, bespoke solutions that closely align with the bank's objectives and requirements.

2. Control and Integration:
   - Having AI capabilities in-house gives banks full control over AI projects, from inception to deployment.
   - It ensures better integration with existing systems and alignment with the bank's data infrastructure and security protocols.

3. Building Internal Expertise:
   - Developing AI expertise internally fosters a deep understanding and knowledge base within the organization.
   - This expertise can be a long-term asset, enabling continuous innovation and adaptation to new challenges and opportunities.

4. Alignment with Organizational Culture:
   - In-house development ensures that AI solutions are developed in a way that is congruent with the bank's values, practices, and culture.
   - This can facilitate smoother adoption and greater acceptance among employees and stakeholders.

5. Data Security and Privacy:
   - Managing AI projects internally can offer greater control over data security and privacy, especially important in the highly regulated banking sector.

6. Long-term Cost Savings:
   - While in-house development may require significant initial investment, it can lead to long-term cost savings by reducing reliance on external vendors.

7. Agility and Flexibility:
   - In-house teams can be more agile and quickly adapt to changing requirements or new insights, offering a competitive advantage in rapidly evolving markets.

Challenges of In-House Development:

- **Resource Intensive:** Developing in-house AI capabilities requires substantial investment in hiring skilled personnel, training, and technology.
- **Time-Consuming:** Building expertise and developing AI solutions from scratch can be time-consuming.
- **Keeping Pace with Technological Advances:** In-house teams must continuously update their skills and knowledge to stay abreast of rapidly advancing AI technologies.

Advantages of Outsourcing AI in Regional Banks

Outsourcing AI development to specialized firms presents a different set of advantages for regional banks, particularly when considering the rapid pace of technological advancement in AI and ML. Here are some of the key benefits:

1. Access to Cutting-Edge Technology and Expertise:
   - Specialized AI firms often have access to the latest technologies and possess deep expertise in AI and ML.
   - Outsourcing allows banks to leverage this advanced know-how without having to develop it in-house.
2. Reduced Development Time:
   - Outsourcing can significantly accelerate the development and deployment of AI solutions.
   - Specialized firms have the experience and resources to execute projects efficiently, reducing the time from concept to implementation.
3. Cost-Effectiveness:
   - Outsourcing can be more cost-effective, especially for banks just beginning their AI journey or for specific projects.
   - It eliminates the need for substantial upfront investments in hiring, training, and technology procurement.
4. Ideal for Starting the AI Journey:

- For banks that are new to AI, outsourcing provides a lower-risk pathway to explore and understand AI's potential.
- It allows banks to gain experience with AI applications before committing to developing in-house capabilities.
5. Flexibility and Scalability:
   - Outsourcing offers the flexibility to scale AI initiatives up or down based on the bank's evolving needs and priorities.
   - This adaptability is valuable in a field that is rapidly evolving and where needs can change quickly.
6. Focus on Core Competencies:
   - By outsourcing AI development, banks can remain focused on their core banking competencies and business goals.
   - This approach allows banks to leverage AI benefits without diverting attention from their primary services and operations.
7. Risk Mitigation:
   - Outsourcing can mitigate the risks associated with the fast-evolving AI technology landscape.
   - It transfers the responsibility of staying up-to-date with AI advancements and maintaining technical proficiency to the external provider.

Adopting a Balanced Approach to AI Development in Regional Banks

A balanced approach to AI development, combining both in-house expertise and outsourced services, can offer regional banks the best of both worlds. This strategy involves developing core AI competencies internally while relying on external firms for specialized or ancillary aspects of AI projects. Here are some key considerations and benefits of this approach:

1. Leveraging Strengths of Both Models:

- The balanced approach capitalizes on the strengths of both in-house development and outsourcing.
- Banks can maintain control over key strategic AI initiatives while tapping into external expertise for cutting-edge technologies or niche applications.

2. Flexibility and Risk Management:
   - This approach offers flexibility in managing resources and mitigates the risk associated with fully committing to either in-house development or complete outsourcing.
   - It allows banks to adjust their strategies based on evolving needs and market conditions.

3. Building In-House Expertise for Core Functions:
   - By developing in-house capabilities for core AI functions, banks can ensure these critical elements align closely with their business goals and data security standards.
   - This approach fosters long-term knowledge accumulation and skill development within the organization.

4. Outsourcing for Specialized Needs:
   - Specialized or complex AI tasks that require niche expertise or advanced technologies can be outsourced to firms with the requisite capabilities.
   - This allows banks to leverage specialized skills that may be impractical or too costly to develop internally.

5. Balancing Cost and Efficiency:
   - The balanced approach can be more cost-effective, combining the cost savings of outsourcing certain aspects with the long-term benefits of in-house development.
   - It also ensures efficient allocation of resources and budget.

6. Ensuring Seamless Integration:

- A critical aspect of this approach is ensuring seamless integration between in-house and outsourced components.
- It requires effective coordination and communication to align the efforts of internal teams and external vendors.
7. Adaptability to Change:
    - This approach enables banks to be more adaptable to technological advancements and changing market demands.
    - It provides the agility to quickly incorporate new technologies or methodologies into their AI initiatives.

Practical Advice:

Adopting a balanced approach to AI development allows regional banks to strategically manage their AI initiatives by combining the control and alignment of in-house development with the expertise and technological advancements of outsourced services. This method offers a pragmatic path to leveraging AI, ensuring that banks can innovate effectively while maintaining a focus on their core competencies and strategic goals.

Integration Strategies for AI and ML in Regional Banks

Implementing AI and ML in regional banks involves various strategic considerations to ensure successful integration and utilization. Here's a comprehensive summary of effective strategies:

1. Seamless Integration with Existing Systems:

- Ensuring AI solutions integrate smoothly with existing banking systems is critical.
- Utilize middleware or APIs for effective integration, requiring meticulous planning and coordination.

2. Collaboration Across Departments:

- AI implementation should involve cross-departmental collaboration, including IT, data science, operations, and compliance teams.
- This ensures AI solutions align with broader business objectives and operational needs.

3. Phased Roll-Out:

- Adopt a phased approach for implementing AI solutions, starting with pilot projects or specific use cases.
- This allows for testing, learning, and making necessary adjustments before broader deployment.

4. Continuous Learning and Adaptation:

- AI infrastructure is dynamic and requires ongoing updates and adaptations to stay relevant and effective.
- Stay abreast of evolving technology trends, regulatory changes, and shifting banking needs.

5. Building a Data-Driven Culture:

- Encourage a culture where data is actively analyzed and used to inform decisions and strategies.
- This cultural shift requires both technological infrastructure and a mindset change throughout the organization.

Summary of Challenges and Considerations:

- Data Privacy and Security:
    - Prioritize protecting customer information and safeguarding against cyber threats.
    - Implement robust security measures and maintain vigilance against evolving cyber risks.
- Ethical AI Implementation:
    - Address algorithmic bias and maintain transparency in AI decision-making.
    - Ethical considerations are vital for maintaining customer trust and regulatory compliance.
- Balancing In-House Development and Outsourcing:

- In-house development offers control and alignment with organizational culture, while outsourcing provides access to advanced technologies and expertise.
- A balanced approach can optimize resources and capabilities.
- Overcoming Technical and Organizational Hurdles:
  - Integrate AI with legacy systems, manage the skill gap, and navigate organizational changes.
  - Continuous training, hiring specialized talent, and effective change management are essential.

Conclusion:

The successful implementation of AI and ML in regional banks is a complex yet rewarding endeavor. It requires navigating various challenges, including data privacy, security, ethical considerations, and technical complexities. Adopting strategies like seamless system integration, cross-departmental collaboration, phased roll-outs, and fostering a data-driven culture are key to this transformation. Banks that effectively navigate these challenges and adopt AI responsibly will enhance their operational efficiency, improve customer experiences, and strengthen their competitive position in the rapidly evolving financial landscape.

Chapter 8: Implementation of AI in Regional Banks

This comprehensive program provides a roadmap for the successful implementation of AI in regional banks, covering every stage from initial planning to ongoing improvement of AI initiatives.

Step 1: Understand the Business Objectives and Gain Support

- **Identify Business Objectives:** Define specific goals and challenges to address with AI, such as enhancing customer service or reducing fraud.
- **Build Executive Support:** Develop a compelling business case showcasing AI's benefits like cost savings and revenue growth to secure top-level buy-in.

Step 2: Assemble a Cross-Functional Team

- **Form a Multidisciplinary Team:** Include data scientists, machine learning engineers, banking experts, IT professionals, and project managers to ensure diverse expertise and collaboration.

Step 3: Build the Data Preparation Infrastructure

- **Data Collection and Preparation:** Focus on gathering and organizing relevant data, ensuring quality, privacy, and security.
- **AI Infrastructure:** Establish necessary infrastructure like cloud resources, computing clusters, and data storage solutions.

Step 4: Define Key Performance Indicators (KPIs)

- **Establish Measurable KPIs:** Set clear metrics to track the success of AI initiatives, including customer satisfaction rates and operational efficiency gains.

Step 5: Pilot Project

- **Start with a Pilot Project:** Choose a manageable AI project to begin with, allowing for learning and risk minimization.

Step 6: AI Use Case Selection and Modeling

- **Select the Right AI Use Case:** Identify use cases that align with your business objectives.
- **Data Modeling and Machine Learning:** Develop and train machine learning models specific to your chosen use case.

Step 7: Technology Stack and Infrastructure

- **Choose AI Tools and Frameworks:** Opt for appropriate AI tools like TensorFlow or PyTorch and cloud platforms for scalability.
- **Infrastructure and Data Pipelines:** Set up the necessary support systems for AI model deployment and banking system integration.

Step 8: Testing, Validation, and Compliance

- **Testing and Validation:** Conduct thorough testing of AI models for accuracy and performance.
- **Regulatory Compliance:** Ensure AI implementations adhere to banking and financial regulations.

Step 9: Deployment, Integration, and Education

- **Deployment and Integration:** Implement AI models into production, ensuring smooth integration.
- **Employee Training and Customer Education:** Educate bank staff and customers about AI-driven services to foster trust and adoption.

Step 10: Monitoring, Maintenance, and Evaluation

- **Monitoring and Maintenance:** Continuously monitor AI systems for performance and maintain models regularly.
- **Evaluate and Scale:** Assess AI's impact on KPIs and consider expanding AI initiatives for broader benefits.

Step 11: Continuous Improvement and Stay Informed

- **Stay Informed:** Keep abreast of the latest in AI, fintech, and regulatory changes.

- **Feedback and Iteration:** Continually gather feedback for iterative improvements to AI systems.

Conclusion: By methodically following these steps, regional banks can effectively navigate their AI implementation journey. From understanding their core objectives to deploying, integrating, and scaling AI solutions, this approach ensures that banks can leverage AI to enhance efficiency, improve customer experiences, and remain competitive in a rapidly evolving financial landscape.

Integration of Artificial Intelligence technology into various business functions has transformed it from a mere curiosity into a fundamental necessity. This chapter delves into a series of practical "recipes" and their expected ROI for five critical domains:

I.   Fraud Detection
II.   Customer Relationship Management (CRM)
III.   Risk Management
IV.   Automation
V.   Compliance

For each use-case, we outline the process in terms of Data Collection and Preparation, Model Development Logic, and Results. Through these sections, we illustrate a structured approach to employing AI and ML for addressing key banking challenges like identity theft, providing a comprehensive blueprint from initial data handling to the realization of tangible outcomes.

- Data Collection and Preparation: This crucial segment lays the groundwork for successful AI and ML applications. It involves gathering and preparing the necessary data, which forms the foundation of any AI/ML model. For instance, in combating identity theft, this step would encompass collecting customer identification data, transaction records, credit reports, digital footprint data, and security incident reports. This phase ensures that the data is accurate, comprehensive, and primed for further analysis, setting a strong foundation for effective model development.
- Model Development Logic: In this section, we delve into the strategies and methodologies for developing AI and ML models. We outline the logical framework and specific algorithms employed to process and analyze the collected data. For example, in addressing identity theft, it would involve applying behavioral analysis, real-time monitoring, fraud detection algorithms, cross-channel analysis, and biometric verification methods. This stage is crucial for

tailoring the AI/ML models to the specific nuances of the banking use-case, ensuring they are accurately tuned to detect and respond to the identified challenges.

- Results: The final section highlights the outcomes and impact of the AI and ML implementation. It assesses the effectiveness of the models in practical scenarios and quantifies their success, such as the reduction in identity theft incidents or fraud-related losses. This part of the chapter not only showcases the benefits and ROI of the AI/ML applications but also reflects on customer confidence and the enhanced security posture of the banks. It underscores the real-world value of AI and ML in banking, demonstrating how these technologies translate into significant operational and financial improvements.

The goal of this chapter is to reveal the "art of the possible" for your bank in AI and then provide the blueprint for implementation to achieve meaningful ROI.

AI has revolutionized the approach to fraud detection in banking. Unlike traditional methods, ML algorithms can process vast volumes of transaction data in real-time, identifying patterns and anomalies that might suggest fraudulent activity. This real-time analysis is crucial in the fast-paced banking environment where quick detection can prevent significant financial losses.

ML algorithms are adept at detecting various types of fraudulent activities. These include:

Transaction Fraud:

Identifying unauthorized or suspicious transactions based on unusual patterns compared to a customer's typical transaction behavior. The utilization of machine learning (ML) and artificial intelligence (AI) in "Transaction Fraud Detection" in banking is a critical development, significantly enhancing the ability to identify and prevent fraudulent activities. These technologies use complex algorithms to analyze transaction patterns and flag irregularities that could *indicate fraudulent behavior.*

Data Collection and Preparation
1. Transaction Data:

- Source: Banking transaction systems, online and mobile banking platforms.
- Content: Details of customer transactions, including time, amount, location, and frequency.

2. Customer Profile Data:

- Source: Bank's customer database.
- Content: Customer account information, transaction history, and behavior patterns.

3. Fraud Incident Reports:

- Source: Fraud detection units, historical fraud databases.

- Content: Information on previously identified fraudulent transactions and patterns.

4. External Data Sources:

- Source: Third-party fraud prevention databases, law enforcement agencies.
- Content: Global fraud trends, blacklisted entities, and high-risk indicators.

5. Device and Access Data:

- Source: Digital banking platforms.
- Content: IP addresses, device information, login patterns, and biometric data.

Model Development Logic

1. Pattern Recognition:

- Utilize ML algorithms (such as neural networks or anomaly detection techniques) to identify unusual transaction patterns that deviate from a customer's normal behavior.

2. Real-time Analysis:

- Develop systems for analyzing transactions in real time, allowing for immediate detection and response to potential fraud.

3. Risk Scoring:

- Assign risk scores to transactions based on various factors, including transaction size, frequency, location, and customer history.

4. Behavioral Analysis:

- Implement behavioral analytics to assess the legitimacy of transactions by comparing them against established customer behavior profiles.

5. Cross-Channel Analysis:

- Analyze transaction data across various channels (ATMs, online banking, mobile apps) to identify coordinated fraud attempts.

Results

The implementation of AI and ML in transaction fraud detection has significantly improved banks' ability to prevent fraud. Banks employing these technologies have reported reductions in fraud losses by up to 30% and increased accuracy in fraud detection. These systems not only provide rapid detection of potential fraud but also reduce false positives, enhancing customer trust and experience. The success of these models depends on continuous data updating, sophisticated algorithm development, and integration with existing banking systems to provide comprehensive fraud protection.

Identity Theft

Detecting applications or transactions that use stolen or fake identity information.

The application of machine learning (ML) and artificial intelligence (AI) in combating "Identity Theft" in banking represents a critical advancement in securing financial transactions and protecting customer information. By leveraging these technologies, banks can significantly enhance their ability to detect and prevent identity theft, safeguarding both their operations and their customers.

Data Collection and Preparation
1. Customer Identification Data:

- Source: Account opening documents, KYC (Know Your Customer) procedures.
- Content: Personal identification details like name, address, social security numbers, biometric data.

2. Transaction Records:

- Source: Banking systems, credit and debit transaction logs.
- Content: Transaction history, patterns, and behaviors associated with customer accounts.

3. Credit Reports and Scores:

- Source: Credit bureaus, third-party credit scoring agencies.
- Content: Credit history, credit inquiries, existing credit accounts, and credit scores.

4. Digital Footprint Data:

- Source: Online banking platforms, social media, internet activity.
- Content: IP addresses, device information, browsing patterns, digital interactions.

5. Security Incident Reports:

- Source: Internal security reports, external cybersecurity databases.
- Content: Information on past incidents of identity theft, fraud trends, security breaches.

Model Development Logic

1. Behavioral Analysis:

- Use ML algorithms to analyze normal customer behavior and flag transactions or activities that deviate from this pattern, indicating potential identity theft.

2. Real-Time Monitoring:

- Develop systems that continuously monitor account activities for signs of unauthorized access or transactions indicative of identity theft.

3. Fraud Detection Algorithms:

- Implement models specifically designed to detect types of fraud commonly associated with identity theft, such as account takeover or application fraud.

4. Cross-Channel Analysis:

- Analyze customer activities across various channels (online, mobile, in-branch) to detect inconsistencies that might signal identity theft.

5. Biometric Verification:

- Integrate biometric verification methods (like fingerprint or facial recognition) to confirm customer identities during transactions.

Results

The integration of AI and ML in the detection and prevention of identity theft has markedly improved banks' security postures. Institutions employing these technologies have noted a significant decrease in identity theft incidents, with some reporting up to a 40% reduction in fraud-related losses. Furthermore, these systems enhance customer confidence by ensuring a secure banking environment. The effectiveness of these solutions relies heavily on the continuous enhancement of ML models, integration of diverse and real-time data sources, and the ability to adapt to evolving identity theft tactics.

Card Fraud

Identifying unauthorized use of credit and debit cards, including skimming and card-not-present fraud.

The incorporation of machine learning (ML) and artificial intelligence (AI) in "Card Fraud Detection" in banking has significantly advanced the security of card-based transactions. These technologies enable banks to analyze transaction patterns in real-time and identify potentially fraudulent activities, thereby protecting customers and reducing financial losses due to fraud.

Data Collection and Preparation
1. Card Transaction Data:

- Source: Card transaction processing systems.
- Content: Transaction details including amount, location, merchant category, time, and frequency of transactions.

2. Customer Account Profiles:

- Source: Bank's customer database.
- Content: Customer's historical transaction data, account usage patterns, and personal information.

3. Security Alerts and Reports:

- Source: Internal security systems, fraud detection units.
- Content: Previously reported instances of card fraud and identified patterns.

4. External Fraud Databases:

- Source: Interbank networks, card associations (like Visa, MasterCard).
- Content: Global fraud trends, blacklisted entities, and reported fraudulent card numbers.

5. Geolocation Data:

- Source: Card transaction details, customer's mobile banking app.

- Content: Location data associated with card transactions and customer's registered devices.

Model Development Logic

1. Anomaly Detection:

    - Utilize ML algorithms (such as clustering techniques or neural networks) to identify unusual transactions that deviate from a customer's typical spending behavior.

2. Pattern Recognition:

    - Develop models that recognize patterns indicative of common card fraud tactics, like sudden spikes in transaction volume or transactions in unusual locations.

3. Real-time Processing:

    - Implement systems capable of analyzing transactions in real-time to detect and respond to potential fraud immediately.

4. Link Analysis:

    - Employ techniques to examine relationships between different transactions, accounts, and geographic locations to uncover coordinated fraud schemes.

5. Risk Scoring:

    - Assign risk scores to transactions based on various indicators of fraud, triggering alerts for high-risk transactions.

Results

The deployment of AI and ML in card fraud detection has resulted in a marked reduction in fraudulent transactions and associated financial losses. Banks utilizing these technologies have reported up to a 50% decrease in card fraud incidents. These systems not only provide enhanced security for card transactions but also improve customer trust and reduce false positives, thereby minimizing unnecessary transaction declines. The success of these systems hinges on their ability to analyze vast datasets in real-time, continuously adapt to new fraud patterns, and integrate seamlessly with existing transaction processing infrastructures.

Insider Fraud

Uncovering fraudulent activities conducted by employees within the bank, often involving the manipulation of accounts or systems.

The application of machine learning (ML) and artificial intelligence (AI) in detecting and preventing "Insider Fraud" within banking institutions marks a significant step forward in internal security measures. These technologies enable banks to monitor and analyze employee actions and behaviors, identifying potential fraudulent activities that might otherwise go unnoticed.

Data Collection and Preparation
1. Employee Access Logs:

- Source: Internal security systems.
- Content: Records of employee access to sensitive systems, databases, and physical areas.

2. Transaction Records:

- Source: Banking transaction processing systems.
- Content: Details of transactions handled or authorized by employees.

3. Communication Data:

- Source: Internal communication systems, emails.
- Content: Employee communications that might contain red flags for fraudulent intentions or collusion.

4. Behavioral Patterns:

- Source: HR records, performance monitoring tools.
- Content: Patterns in employee performance, behavior anomalies, discrepancies between reported activities and system logs.

5. Audit Trails:

- Source: Internal audit systems.

- Content: Historical data of employee actions within banking systems for audit and review.

Model Development Logic

1. Anomaly Detection:

- Use ML algorithms to detect unusual patterns in employee behavior or access patterns that deviate from their regular work profile or peer group activities.

2. Predictive Modeling:

- Develop predictive models to identify risk indicators associated with insider fraud, such as unusual access patterns or transaction activities.

3. Network Analysis:

- Apply network analysis to map and analyze relationships and interactions among employees, identifying potential collusion or insider networks.

4. Behavioral Analytics:

- Implement behavioral analytics to understand normal employee behavior and flag actions that fall outside these parameters.

5. Risk Scoring:

- Assign risk scores to employee actions based on various factors, including access levels, transaction values, and anomalies detected.

Results

Incorporating AI and ML into insider fraud detection strategies has led to a more proactive and effective approach to internal banking security. Banks that have implemented these technologies report a significant reduction in instances of insider fraud, with some observing up to a 40% decrease in related losses. These systems not only aid in the early detection of fraudulent activities but also act as a deterrent for potential insider threats. Their effectiveness relies on continuous analysis of comprehensive data sets, sophisticated algorithmic development, and integration with existing internal monitoring systems.

Money Laundering

Recognizing patterns consistent with money laundering, such as complex layers of financial transactions designed to conceal the origin of funds.

The deployment of machine learning (ML) and artificial intelligence (AI) in "Money Laundering Detection" within banking institutions is a pivotal advancement in combating financial crime. These technologies enable banks to analyze vast amounts of transaction data, identify suspicious patterns, and take timely action to prevent money laundering activities.

Data Collection and Preparation
1. Customer Transaction Data:

- Source: Banking transaction systems.
- Content: Details of customer transactions, including amount, frequency, beneficiary details, and cross-border transfers.

2. Account Holder Profiles:

- Source: Bank's customer database.
- Content: Customer identification information, account history, and associated risk profiles.

3. Suspicious Activity Reports (SARs):

- Source: Compliance department, previous investigations.
- Content: Historical data on reported suspicious activities and outcomes of investigations.

4. Global Watchlists and Sanctions Lists:

- Source: Government and international regulatory bodies.
- Content: Lists of individuals, entities, and countries subject to sanctions or flagged for financial crimes.

5. External Transaction Databases:

- Source: Interbank networks, third-party financial crime databases.

- Content: Global transaction data, trends in money laundering activities, and typologies.

Model Development Logic

1. Pattern Recognition:

   - Use ML algorithms to identify patterns of transactions that are indicative of money laundering, such as structuring, layering, or unusual cross-border activities.

2. Anomaly Detection:

   - Implement systems to detect anomalies in transaction behaviors that deviate from the norm for a particular customer or account type.

3. Risk Scoring:

   - Assign risk scores to transactions and customers based on a range of indicators, including transaction size, frequency, and the risk level of counterparties.

4. Network Analysis:

   - Apply network analysis techniques to uncover relationships and flows of funds between accounts that may indicate money laundering schemes.

5. Behavioral Monitoring:

   - Continuously monitor customer behaviors and transactions to detect changes that might signal money laundering activities.

Results

The integration of AI and ML in money laundering detection has significantly increased the efficiency and effectiveness of banks' anti-money laundering (AML) efforts. Banks employing these technologies have experienced a marked improvement in the detection of suspicious activities, with some reporting up to a 50% increase in the identification of potential money laundering cases. These systems not only enhance the ability to detect complex laundering schemes but also reduce false positives, thereby optimizing the allocation of investigative resources. The success of these models hinges on their ability to process large datasets, adapt to evolving laundering tactics, and integrate seamlessly with banks' existing AML frameworks.

II Customer Relationship Management (CRM) Domain:

This section focuses on the transformative impact of Machine Learning (ML) on Customer Relationship Management (CRM) in the banking sector. It explores how ML can enhance CRM strategies, from segmenting customers for targeted marketing to predicting customer churn. The integration of ML into CRM systems marks a significant shift from traditional, rule-based CRM approaches. ML algorithms can analyze vast amounts of customer data - from transaction histories to online behavior patterns - to gain deeper insights into customer preferences and behaviors. This data-driven approach enables banks to create more effective CRM strategies that are responsive to individual customer needs and market dynamics.

Tailored Product Recommendations

A "tailored product recommendation" machine learning (ML) model in a banking context is designed to suggest financial products and services that are most relevant to individual customers based on their unique needs and behaviors. Implementing such a model involves several steps, from data collection to the application of specific algorithms.

Data Collection and Preparation
Customer Data:

- Source: Gathered from bank's internal systems (core banking system, CRM, etc.).
- Content: Includes customer demographics (age, gender, occupation), contact information, and account types.

Transactional Data:

- Source: Transaction processing systems.
- Content: Details of transactions (amounts, dates, types of transactions like deposits, withdrawals, etc.).

Interaction Data:

- Source: Customer service interactions, website and app usage data, and feedback forms.
- Content: Customer queries, complaints, feedback, and navigation patterns on digital platforms.

Credit History:

- Source: Credit bureaus or internal credit scoring systems.
- Content: Credit scores, loan repayment history, existing liabilities.

Marketing Response Data:

- Source: Marketing campaign management tools.
- Content: Customer responses to previous marketing campaigns (clicks, conversions, etc.).

Model Development Logic
Data Preprocessing:

- Clean and preprocess the data to handle missing values, outliers, and normalize the data.
- Feature engineering to extract meaningful attributes from raw data (e.g., average transaction size, frequency of branch visits).

Customer Segmentation:

- Apply clustering techniques (like K-means) to segment customers into distinct groups based on their behaviors and characteristics.

Recommendation Engine:

- Implement algorithms like collaborative filtering, content-based filtering, or hybrid methods.
- Collaborative filtering can suggest products that similar customers have found valuable.

- Content-based filtering recommends products that match the customer's profile (e.g., high-yield savings accounts for customers with large balances).

Personalization:

- Use predictive analytics to predict future customer needs based on past behaviors (e.g., predicting a need for a home loan based on increasing savings patterns).
- Personalize recommendations by combining the outputs of the segmentation and predictive models.

Feedback Loop:

- Incorporate a feedback mechanism to refine recommendations based on customer responses to previous suggestions.

Model Deployment and Monitoring

- The model should be integrated into the bank's customer-facing platforms (website, mobile app) and customer relationship management systems.
- Regularly monitor and update the model to adapt to changing customer behaviors and preferences.

Ethical and Privacy Considerations

- Ensure compliance with data privacy laws and regulations (like GDPR).
- Implement transparent data usage policies and seek customer consent where necessary.

Results

Specific increases in sales vary. For instance, some reports suggest that banks and financial institutions have observed a 10-30% increase in sales for certain products following the implementation of personalized recommendation systems.

A tailored product recommendation system in banking harnesses ML to provide personalized financial product suggestions to customers. It requires a robust pipeline of data collection, preprocessing, model development, and constant refinement to ensure relevancy and effectiveness. Such models not only enhance customer satisfaction but also drive business growth by matching the right products with the right customers.

Segmenting Customers for Personalizing Marketing:

Data-Driven Segmentation: ML algorithms excel in segmenting customers into distinct groups based on various parameters like spending habits, income levels, life stages, and more. This segmentation allows banks to understand the unique characteristics of each group, tailoring products and services to suit their specific needs.

The implementation of machine learning (ML) and artificial intelligence (AI) in "Customer Segmentation for Personalized Marketing" in banking is a strategic approach to tailor marketing efforts and improve customer engagement. By leveraging these technologies, banks can segment customers into distinct groups based on shared characteristics, enabling more targeted and effective marketing strategies.

Data Collection and Preparation
1. Customer Demographic Data:

- Source: Account opening forms, customer profiles.
- Content: Age, gender, income level, marital status, occupation, and geographic location.

2. Transaction and Account Data:

- Source: Banking systems.
- Content: Transaction history, account types, frequency of transactions, average transaction values, and account balances.

3. Digital Interaction Data:

- Source: Online banking platforms, mobile apps.
- Content: Website visit patterns, mobile app usage, click-through rates, and responses to digital marketing campaigns.

4. Customer Feedback:

- Source: Surveys, feedback forms, customer service interactions.

- Content: Customer preferences, satisfaction levels, product and service feedback.

5. Social Media Data:

- Source: Social media platforms.
- Content: Social media interactions, likes, comments, shares related to banking products and services.

Model Development Logic
1. Cluster Analysis:

- Utilize unsupervised ML algorithms like K-means clustering to group customers into segments based on similarities in their data profiles.

2. Behavioral Segmentation:

- Analyze transaction patterns and digital interactions to segment customers based on their behavior, such as spending habits or digital banking usage.

3. Demographic Segmentation:

- Group customers based on demographic data to create segments for targeted marketing campaigns tailored to specific age groups, income levels, or geographic locations.

4. Psychographic Segmentation:

- Consider customers' lifestyles, values, and attitudes for segmentation, inferred from transaction data and social media interactions.

5. Predictive Analytics:

- Use predictive models to forecast future customer behaviors and preferences, enabling proactive and personalized marketing strategies.

Results
Integrating AI and ML in customer segmentation for personalized marketing has led to significantly improved marketing efficacy in

banking. Banks implementing these techniques report enhanced customer engagement, higher conversion rates, and increased ROI from marketing campaigns, with some experiencing up to a 30% improvement in customer response rates. These systems allow banks to deliver relevant and personalized marketing messages, fostering stronger customer relationships and better satisfaction. The success of these models depends on the comprehensiveness and quality of the data used, the sophistication of the ML algorithms, and the alignment of segmentation strategies with overall marketing goals.

Dynamic Product Recommendations:

ML models can suggest relevant financial products or services to customers based on their transaction history and preferences. This not only enhances the customer experience but also opens up cross-selling and up-selling opportunities for the bank.

Incorporating machine learning (ML) and artificial intelligence (AI) for "Dynamic Product Recommendations" in banking has revolutionized how financial products are offered to customers. These technologies enable banks to provide real-time, personalized product suggestions, enhancing customer experiences and increasing conversion rates.

Data Collection and Preparation
1. Customer Transaction Data:

- Source: Banking transaction systems.
- Content: Details of customer transactions including amounts, types of transactions, frequency, and historical data.

2. Customer Account Information:

- Source: Bank's customer relationship management (CRM) system.
- Content: Account types, balances, duration of the relationship with the bank, and other account-specific details.

3. Customer Interaction Data:

- Source: Online and mobile banking platforms, customer service interactions.
- Content: Queries raised by customers, responses to previous product offers, and engagement with online banking tools.

4. Demographic and Psychographic Data:

- Source: Account opening forms, marketing surveys.
- Content: Age, income, occupation, lifestyle preferences, and financial goals.

5. External Market Data:

- Source: Market research reports, third-party financial data aggregators.
- Content: Economic trends, interest rates, market demand for various financial products.

Model Development Logic

1. Personalization Algorithms:

    - Utilize AI algorithms to analyze customer data and predict products that best suit individual customer needs, based on their transaction history and interactions.

2. Real-Time Recommendation Engines:

    - Implement systems that deliver product recommendations in real time, for instance, during a customer's online banking session or through a mobile banking app.

3. Cross-Selling and Upselling Techniques:

    - Develop models that identify opportunities for cross-selling (offering complementary products) and upselling (suggesting premium products) based on customer profiles and behaviors.

4. Customer Lifetime Value Prediction:

    - Use predictive analytics to estimate the lifetime value of customers, targeting those most likely to respond positively to specific product offerings.

5. Feedback Loop Integration:

    - Incorporate a feedback mechanism to refine recommendations based on customer responses, continuously improving the relevance of the suggestions.

Results

The deployment of AI and ML for dynamic product recommendations has led to a more personalized and efficient marketing approach in banking. Financial institutions that have adopted these technologies report substantial increases in product uptake, with some experiencing up to a 40% improvement in conversion rates for recommended products. This approach not only enhances customer satisfaction by providing relevant offers but also boosts the bank's revenue and cross-selling opportunities. The effectiveness of these models hinges on continuous data analysis, adaptive learning from customer feedback, and seamless integration with digital banking platforms.

Churn Prediction Models:

One of the significant applications of ML in CRM is predicting customer churn. By analyzing patterns in historical data, ML models can identify early warning signs of customers who are likely to leave. These indicators might include decreased transaction frequency, lower engagement levels, or complaints.

The implementation of machine learning (ML) and artificial intelligence (AI) for "Churn Prediction" in banking is a strategic move towards retaining customers and enhancing overall customer satisfaction. By leveraging these technologies, banks can proactively identify customers who are at risk of leaving and take action to address their concerns, thus reducing churn rates.

Data Collection and Preparation
1. Customer Account Data:

- Source: Bank's customer database.
- Content: Account types, tenure, balances, and historical data on account usage.

2. Transaction History:

- Source: Transaction processing systems.
- Content: Frequency, volume, and types of transactions, including deposits, withdrawals, and online transactions.

3. Customer Interaction Records:

- Source: Customer service systems, CRM platforms.
- Content: Records of customer inquiries, complaints, service requests, and their resolutions.

4. Digital Engagement Metrics:

- Source: Online and mobile banking analytics.
- Content: Login frequency, usage patterns of digital services, and interactions with online tools and features.

5. Customer Feedback and Surveys:

- Source: Feedback forms, surveys.
- Content: Customer satisfaction scores, feedback on services, and reasons for dissatisfaction if any.

Model Development Logic

1. Predictive Analytics:

- Employ predictive modeling techniques to analyze customer data and identify patterns or indicators that signal an increased likelihood of churn.

2. Behavioral Analysis:

- Analyze customer behaviors, such as reduced transaction frequency or changes in account usage, which often precede account closure.

3. Sentiment Analysis:

- Implement NLP techniques to gauge customer sentiment from interaction records and feedback, identifying dissatisfaction or service issues.

4. Risk Scoring:

- Assign churn risk scores to customers based on various predictive factors, enabling targeted intervention strategies for high-risk individuals.

5. Customer Segmentation:

- Segment customers based on churn risk and other characteristics, tailoring retention strategies to different segments.

Results

Incorporating AI and ML in churn prediction has empowered banks to significantly reduce churn rates, with some institutions reporting up to a 30% reduction in customer attrition. These systems enable banks to understand customer needs better, predict potential dissatisfaction, and proactively address issues, enhancing customer loyalty and retention. The success of churn prediction models is dependent on the comprehensive analysis of customer data, integration of diverse data sources, and the ability to act on the insights generated in a timely manner.

Proactive Customer Retention Strategies:

Armed with insights from churn prediction models, banks can develop proactive strategies to retain customers at risk of churning. This might involve offering personalized incentives, addressing service issues, or engaging with customers through targeted communication.

Incorporating machine learning (ML) and artificial intelligence (AI) in "Proactive Customer Retention" strategies in banking is a forward-thinking approach to maintain and strengthen the customer base. These technologies enable banks to anticipate customer needs, address potential issues before they escalate, and enhance overall customer satisfaction, leading to increased loyalty and retention.

Incorporating machine learning (ML) and artificial intelligence (AI) in "Proactive Customer Retention" strategies in banking is a forward-thinking approach to maintain and strengthen the customer base. These technologies enable banks to anticipate customer needs, address potential issues before they escalate, and enhance overall customer satisfaction, leading to increased loyalty and retention.

Data Collection and Preparation
1. Customer Interaction Data:

- Source: CRM systems, customer service interactions.
- Content: Details of customer inquiries, complaints, feedback, and interactions with bank representatives.

2. Transaction History:

- Source: Banking systems.
- Content: Types and frequency of transactions, account activity patterns, and usage of banking services.

3. Customer Satisfaction Surveys:

- Source: Survey tools, feedback forms.
- Content: Customer satisfaction levels, preferences, and areas of concern.

4. Behavioral Data:

- Source: Digital banking platforms, mobile apps.
- Content: Usage patterns, feature engagement, and digital interaction behaviors.

5. Demographic and Psychographic Information:

- Source: Account opening records, marketing research.
- Content: Age, income, lifestyle preferences, and financial goals.

Model Development Logic

1. Predictive Analytics:

- Utilize ML models to predict the likelihood of customer churn based on historical data and interaction patterns.

2. Sentiment Analysis:

- Apply NLP techniques to analyze customer feedback and communication, gauging sentiment and identifying dissatisfaction.

3. Personalization Algorithms:

- Develop systems that offer personalized banking experiences, such as tailored product recommendations or customized advice, based on individual customer data.

4. Early Warning Systems:

- Implement models that flag early signs of customer disengagement or potential dissatisfaction, triggering proactive outreach.

5. Customer Value Analysis:

- Analyze customers' lifetime value and profitability to prioritize retention efforts for high-value customers.

Results

Adopting AI and ML for proactive customer retention has enabled banks to achieve significant improvements in customer loyalty, with some reporting up to a 25% increase in retention rates. These strategies help banks to not only retain existing customers but also turn them into long-term, satisfied clients. Success in proactive customer retention hinges on the effective use of data analytics to understand customer needs, timely and personalized engagement, and the continuous adaptation of strategies based on customer feedback and changing behaviors.

Investment Recommendations

An "investment recommendation" machine learning (ML) model in a bank is designed to offer personalized investment advice by aligning financial products with individual client profiles, investment goals, and market conditions. This model aims to enhance customer satisfaction and can potentially lead to an increase in investment product sales.

Data Collection and Preparation
1. Client Profile Data:

- Source: CRM system and account management systems of the bank.
- Content: Includes demographics, investment experience, risk tolerance, and financial goals of clients.

2. Transactional and Account Data:

- Source: Investment transaction systems.
- Content: Details of historical transactions, current holdings, and account performance.

3. Market Data:

- Source: Financial market data providers.
- Content: Includes stock prices, bond yields, economic indicators, and historical market trends.

4. Client Interaction Data:

- Source: Customer service records and digital interaction logs.
- Content: Records client inquiries and feedback on previous investment advice.

5. Regulatory Compliance Data:

- Source: Internal compliance databases.
- Content: Ensures client suitability for certain investments based on regulatory standards.

Model Development Logic
1.   Risk Profiling:

- Classification algorithms to assess clients' risk tolerance and categorize them accordingly.

2. Investment Matching:

- Recommendation algorithms to match investment products to client risk profiles.

3. Portfolio Optimization:

- Optimization algorithms suggest portfolios that balance risk and return effectively.

4. Predictive Analytics:

- Predictive models forecast market trends and their potential impacts on investments.

5. Personalization:

- Tailoring investment suggestions based on both financial and behavioral data of clients.

Results

Implementing an ML-based investment recommendation system in banking has the potential to significantly enhance the customer advisory experience and increase investment product sales. Banks that have adopted such systems report a range of sales increases, typically between 10% to 40%. The exact benefit depends on several factors, including the system's effectiveness, integration into the bank's advisory process, and the nature of the client base. Ultimately, the success of these models is tied to the quality of data, algorithm sophistication, and ethical considerations, including adherence to financial regulations and data privacy standards.

III Risk-Management Domain:

This section examines how Artificial Intelligence (AI) and Machine Learning (ML) are revolutionizing risk management in regional banks. It explores the development of advanced credit scoring models, the identification and mitigation of various risks, and presents case studies highlighting the successful application of these technologies.

Credit Scoring

Traditional credit scoring methods, often based on static criteria and historical data, are being enhanced with ML models. These models incorporate a broader range of data points, including non-traditional and real-time data, to assess creditworthiness more accurately and inclusively. ML algorithms can detect subtle patterns and correlations in the data that might be missed by traditional models, leading to more nuanced credit risk assessments. This approach enables banks to reduce defaults and make informed lending decisions.

The integration of machine learning (ML) and artificial intelligence (AI) into "Credit Scoring" systems in banking is transforming the traditional credit assessment process. These advanced technologies enable banks to analyze a broader range of data more accurately and efficiently, offering a more comprehensive and nuanced view of a borrower's creditworthiness.

Data Collection and Preparation

1. Financial History:

- Source: Banking records, credit bureaus.
- Content: Credit card usage, loan history, payment records, defaults, and bankruptcies.

2. Income and Employment Data:

- Source: Customer application forms, employment verification processes.
- Content: Income level, employment stability, and career progression.

3. Transactional Data:

- Source: Customer bank accounts.
- Content: Account balances, deposit and withdrawal patterns, and fund management.

4. Demographic Information:

- Source: Application forms, KYC documents.
- Content: Age, marital status, number of dependents, education level.

5. Alternative Data:

- Source: Utility bills, rent payments, online transactions.
- Content: Data that may not be traditionally used in credit scoring but can provide insights into a customer's financial behavior.

Model Development Logic

1. Predictive Modeling:

- Utilize ML algorithms to analyze traditional and alternative data sources, predicting the likelihood of loan repayment.

2. Risk Assessment:

- Develop models that assess various risk factors, assigning a risk score based on the customer's financial history and behavior.

3. Behavioral Analysis:

- Incorporate analysis of transactional behaviors to identify patterns that may indicate financial stability or risk.

4. Customized Scoring Models:

- Create tailored credit scoring models for different customer segments or product types, enhancing accuracy and relevance.

5. Continuous Learning:

- Implement systems that continually learn from new data, adapting and improving credit scoring accuracy over time.

Results

The application of AI and ML in credit scoring has led to more inclusive and fair credit decisions, with some banks reporting up to a 20% reduction in defaults while expanding credit access. These technologies enable a more dynamic and responsive approach to credit risk assessment, taking into account a wider array of variables than traditional models. The effectiveness of AI-powered credit scoring models is heavily reliant on the quality and diversity of data used, as well as the sophistication of the algorithms in capturing nuanced patterns and relationships within the data.

Credit Risks

A "loan credit risk" machine learning (ML) model in a bank is a vital tool for assessing the probability of loan defaults. This sophisticated model leverages various data points to make informed lending decisions, manage risk effectively, and minimize financial losses due to loan defaults.

Data Collection and Preparation
1. Borrower's Financial Profile:

- Source: Loan application forms, credit bureaus.
- Content: Credit scores, income details, employment history, existing loans and debts.

2. Loan Transaction Data:

- Source: Bank's internal loan processing systems.
- Content: Loan amounts, terms, interest rates, repayment history.

3. Economic Indicators:

- Source: Financial market data services, economic research bodies.
- Content: Market interest rates, inflation rates, unemployment data, and other economic health indicators.

4. Behavioral Data:

- Source: Bank's internal transaction databases.
- Content: Account activity, payment histories, overdraft occurrences.

5. Collateral Information:

- Source: Property records, asset valuation databases.
- Content: Information on collateral value for secured loans.

Model Development Logic
1. Risk Scoring:

- Utilize classification models like logistic regression, random forests, or neural networks to predict default likelihood based on the borrower's financial data.

2. Feature Engineering:

- Develop features that capture risk factors effectively, such as debt-to-income ratios, loan-to-value ratios, and historical payment behaviors.

3. Segmentation:

- Cluster borrowers into different risk groups to tailor risk assessment and loan offerings appropriately.

4. Predictive Analysis:

- Implement models to predict future economic shifts and their impact on loan default rates.

5. Model Testing and Validation:

- Rigorously test the model using historical data to ensure its accuracy in predicting loan defaults.

Results

The deployment of a loan credit risk ML model can significantly improve a bank's ability to assess and manage loan risks. Banks utilizing such models have reported a notable reduction in default rates. For instance, a case study revealed that after implementing a comprehensive credit risk ML model, a regional bank experienced a 20% reduction in loan defaults within the first year of deployment. This marked improvement in loan quality underscores the model's effectiveness in enhancing the bank's lending decisions, risk management practices, and overall financial stability. The success of these models hinges on the quality and comprehensiveness of the data, the sophistication of the algorithms, and strict adherence to regulatory and ethical standards, including fair lending practices

Identifying Risks:

AI and ML extend beyond credit scoring to encompass a wider spectrum of risk management activities.

The utilization of machine learning (ML) and artificial intelligence (AI) in "Identifying Risks" in banking is a groundbreaking approach to enhancing risk management strategies. These technologies enable banks to proactively identify and mitigate a wide range of financial, operational, and compliance-related risks.

Data Collection and Preparation

1. Transaction Data:

- Source: Transaction processing systems.
- Content: Patterns, anomalies, and trends in customer transactions.

2. Customer Interaction Records:

- Source: CRM systems, customer service logs.
- Content: Customer queries, complaints, and feedback, potentially signaling operational issues.

3. Market and Economic Data:

- Source: Financial market data providers, economic research.
- Content: Market trends, economic indicators, and external factors affecting risk.

4. Regulatory Compliance Reports:

- Source: Internal compliance departments, regulatory bodies.
- Content: Past compliance issues, regulatory changes, and benchmarks.

5. Internal Audit Reports:

- Source: Internal audit department.
- Content: Findings from previous audits, identifying areas of risk within bank operations.

1. Predictive Analysis:

- Employ predictive modeling to forecast potential risks based on historical data and emerging trends.

2. Anomaly Detection:

- Implement anomaly detection algorithms to identify unusual patterns or transactions that could indicate fraud or operational risk.

3. Risk Scoring Models:

- Develop scoring systems to quantify risk levels for various aspects of banking operations, including credit, market, and operational risks.

4. Sentiment Analysis:

- Apply NLP techniques to analyze customer feedback and market opinions, which can provide early warning signs of reputational risk.

5. Regulatory Compliance Monitoring:

- Utilize AI to continuously monitor transactions and operations against regulatory requirements, identifying potential compliance risks.

Results

Integrating AI and ML in risk identification processes has significantly enhanced the ability of banks to anticipate and mitigate risks. Banks employing these technologies have reported more efficient risk detection and management, with some experiencing up to a 30% improvement in identifying and addressing risks proactively. These systems provide a more dynamic risk management approach, capable of adapting to changing market conditions and emerging threats. Success in this area depends on the continuous analysis of a wide range of data, the ability to interpret complex patterns, and the integration of these insights into the bank's risk management strategy.

Market and Operational Risk:

ML models can analyze market trends and predict potential market disruptions, helping banks in mitigating market risks. They can also identify inefficiencies and vulnerabilities in operational processes.

Incorporating machine learning (ML) and artificial intelligence (AI) to assess "Market and Operational Risk" in banking is a transformative approach to managing the complex and dynamic nature of these risks. These technologies enable banks to gain deeper insights into market fluctuations and internal operational efficiencies, thereby enhancing risk management strategies.

Data Collection and Preparation
1. Market Data:

- Source: Financial markets, trading platforms.
- Content: Stock prices, interest rates, currency exchange rates, commodity prices, and market indices.

2. Economic Indicators:

- Source: Government reports, economic research institutions.
- Content: GDP growth rates, inflation, unemployment rates, and economic policy changes.

3. Operational Data:

- Source: Internal banking systems.
- Content: Transaction volumes, process workflows, error rates, and system downtime.

4. Customer and Transaction Records:

- Source: CRM and transaction processing systems.
- Content: Customer profiles, transaction types, frequencies, and anomalies.

5. Internal Audit Reports:

- Source: Internal audit department.

- Content: Historical data on operational failures, compliance breaches, or internal fraud.

Model Development Logic

1. Predictive Modeling:

- Employ ML algorithms to analyze market data and predict future market trends, assisting in understanding market risk exposure.

2. Stress Testing:

- Implement stress testing models that simulate various adverse market scenarios to assess the impact on the bank's financial position.

3. Operational Efficiency Analysis:

- Utilize AI to monitor and analyze operational processes, identifying inefficiencies or areas prone to error that contribute to operational risk.

4. Anomaly Detection:

- Develop anomaly detection systems to identify unusual patterns in operational data that could indicate system failures or process inefficiencies.

5. Risk Scoring and Mitigation Strategies:

- Create risk scoring models that quantify market and operational risks, facilitating the prioritization of mitigation strategies.

Results

Adopting AI and ML for assessing market and operational risks enables banks to proactively manage these risks with greater accuracy and efficiency. Banks have reported significant improvements in risk detection and response times, with some experiencing up to a 20% reduction in losses due to enhanced market and operational risk management. The effectiveness of these models depends on the continuous monitoring and analysis of a wide array of data, the accuracy of predictive algorithms, and the integration of risk insights into strategic decision-making processes.

Compliance Risk:

AI tools streamline the process of monitoring and ensuring compliance with various regulatory requirements, reducing the risk of non-compliance penalties.

Integrating machine learning (ML) and artificial intelligence (AI) into "Compliance Risk" management in banking is a strategic move towards enhancing regulatory adherence and minimizing the risk of non-compliance. This innovative approach enables banks to navigate the complex and ever-evolving regulatory landscape more effectively and efficiently.

Data Collection and Preparation
1. Regulatory Requirements Data:

- Source: Regulatory bodies, legal updates.
- Content: Current and upcoming regulations, compliance guidelines, and legal requirements in the banking sector.

2. Transaction Records:

- Source: Banking transaction systems.
- Content: Details of customer transactions including types, amounts, and frequencies.

3. Customer Due Diligence Information:

- Source: KYC (Know Your Customer) processes.
- Content: Customer identification documents, background checks, and risk categorization.

4. Internal Policy Documents:

- Source: Bank's internal policy database.
- Content: Bank's internal compliance policies, procedures, and codes of conduct.

5. Audit and Inspection Reports:

- Source: Internal and external audit agencies.

- Content: Previous audit findings, identified compliance issues, and recommendations.

Model Development Logic

1. Regulatory Monitoring:

   - Develop AI systems to continuously monitor and interpret regulatory changes, ensuring that the bank's practices stay in alignment with current laws and guidelines.

2. Transaction Monitoring:

   - Implement ML algorithms to analyze transaction data, detecting patterns and activities that may indicate non-compliance, such as money laundering or fraudulent transactions.

3. Risk Assessment Models:

   - Utilize AI to assess and score compliance risks associated with various banking activities, customer profiles, and transactions.

4. Automated Compliance Checks:

   - Deploy automated systems to perform regular compliance checks on customer accounts, transactions, and internal processes.

5. Reporting and Alerting Mechanisms:

   - Integrate reporting tools that automatically generate compliance reports and alert relevant departments of potential compliance issues.

Results

The adoption of AI and ML in compliance risk management has resulted in more robust and dynamic compliance processes, with some banks reporting up to a 25% reduction in compliance-related costs. These technologies enhance the accuracy and timeliness of compliance monitoring, reduce the manual burden on compliance teams, and improve the bank's overall ability to respond to regulatory changes. The success of these models depends on the comprehensive and up-to-date regulatory data, accurate risk assessment algorithms, and seamless integration of these systems into the bank's compliance framework.

Liquidity Risk:

AI models can forecast future cash flow scenarios, helping banks manage their liquidity more effectively.

Incorporating machine learning (ML) and artificial intelligence (AI) in managing "Liquidity Risk" in banking represents a significant advancement in financial risk management. By employing these technologies, banks can better predict and manage scenarios that could impact their liquidity, ensuring financial stability and regulatory compliance.

Data Collection and Preparation
1. Cash Flow Data:

- Source: Financial statements, transaction systems.
- Content: Incoming and outgoing cash flows, including loan disbursements, deposit withdrawals, and investment activities.

2. Market Data:

Source: Financial markets, trading platforms.

- Content: Market liquidity indicators, interest rates, and economic trends that influence liquidity.

3. Historical Liquidity Data:

- Source: Internal financial records.
- Content: Historical patterns and trends in liquidity levels, including periods of stress.

4. Customer Account Data:

- Source: Banking systems.
- Content: Deposit levels, withdrawal patterns, and customer behavior related to liquidity demands.

5. Regulatory Requirements:

- Source: Regulatory bodies, compliance departments.

- Content: Liquidity coverage ratios, capital requirements, and other regulatory standards related to liquidity.

Model Development Logic

1. Predictive Analysis:

- Utilize ML algorithms to forecast future cash flow scenarios and liquidity requirements based on historical data and market trends.

2. Stress Testing:

- Implement stress-testing models that simulate various adverse market and operational scenarios to assess their impact on liquidity.

3. Real-Time Monitoring:

- Develop systems for real-time monitoring of liquidity levels, enabling quick responses to any potential liquidity crises.

4. Scenario Analysis:

- Conduct scenario analyses to understand the potential impact of various market and operational events on liquidity.

5. Risk Scoring Models:

- Create risk scoring models that quantify liquidity risk, assisting in proactive risk management and decision-making.

Results

The integration of AI and ML in liquidity risk management enables banks to proactively and efficiently manage their liquidity positions. Banks using these technologies have reported improvements in their ability to anticipate liquidity needs and comply with regulatory standards, with some experiencing a marked reduction in liquidity-related risks. The effectiveness of these systems hinges on accurate and timely data analysis, sophisticated predictive models, and the ability to integrate insights into liquidity management strategies.

Capital Optimization

Leveraging machine learning (ML) and artificial intelligence (AI) in "Capital Optimization" is transforming how banks manage and allocate their capital resources. These technologies enable more precise forecasting, risk assessment, and resource allocation, ensuring that banks can efficiently meet regulatory requirements while also pursuing profitable ventures.

Data Collection and Preparation
1. Financial Statement Data:

- Source: Bank's internal financial records.
- Content: Balance sheets, income statements, cash flow statements.

2. Regulatory Capital Requirements:

- Source: Regulatory bodies (e.g., Basel Committee).
- Content: Minimum capital requirements, liquidity thresholds, stress testing scenarios.

3. Market and Credit Risk Data:

- Source: Financial markets, internal risk management systems.
- Content: Market volatility data, credit exposure, default probabilities.

4. Operational Performance Metrics:

- Source: Internal performance tracking systems.
- Content: Revenue streams, operational costs, return on investments (ROI).

5. Economic Indicators:

- Source: Economic research, government publications.
- Content: GDP growth, inflation rates, economic forecasts.

Model Development Logic
1. Risk-Weighted Asset (RWA) Optimization:

- Utilize ML to analyze risk factors and optimize the allocation of capital against risk-weighted assets, aligning with regulatory requirements.

2. Capital Adequacy Forecasting:

- Implement predictive models to forecast future capital requirements under various market conditions and operational scenarios.

3. Investment Portfolio Optimization:

- Apply AI algorithms to maximize returns on the bank's investment portfolio while maintaining the necessary capital ratios.

4. Stress Testing and Scenario Analysis:

- Conduct AI-driven stress tests and scenario analyses to assess the impact of adverse market conditions on the bank's capital position.

5. Operational Efficiency Improvements:

- Leverage AI to identify areas for operational cost reduction, thereby freeing up capital for other uses.

Results

The adoption of AI and ML in capital optimization has led to more informed decision-making, improved compliance with regulatory capital requirements, and enhanced return on capital. Banks utilizing these technologies have reported improved capital efficiency, with some experiencing up to a 20% improvement in capital utilization. The effectiveness of these models is contingent on accurate forecasting, the ability to adapt to changing market conditions, and strategic alignment with the bank's overall business objectives.

Know Your Customer

Implementing machine learning (ML) and artificial intelligence (AI) in "Know Your Customer" (KYC) protocols is revolutionizing the way banks manage customer due diligence and compliance. These technologies streamline the KYC process, enhance accuracy in customer identification, and strengthen anti-money laundering (AML) efforts.

Data Collection and Preparation

1. Personal Identification Data:

- Source: Customer application forms, government-issued IDs.
- Content: Names, addresses, dates of birth, identification numbers.

2. Financial Background Information:

- Source: Credit bureaus, financial statements.
- Content: Credit history, source of funds, financial associations.

3. Transaction History:

- Source: Banking systems.
- Content: Account transactions, transfer histories, and payment patterns.

4. Public and Legal Records:

- Source: Public databases, court records.
- Content: Legal disputes, sanctions lists, politically exposed persons (PEPs).

5. Social Media and Online Presence:

- Source: Internet, social media platforms.
- Content: Online behavior, social networks, professional affiliations.

Model Development Logic

1. Automated Document Verification:

- Utilize AI to automate the verification of identification documents, reducing manual errors and speeding up the KYC process.

2. Risk Profiling:

- Implement ML algorithms to assess the risk level of customers based on their financial background, transaction behavior, and other relevant data.

3. Behavioral Analysis:

- Analyze transaction patterns using AI to identify unusual activities that might indicate money laundering or other financial crimes.

4. Ongoing Monitoring:

- Develop systems for continuous monitoring of customer activities to ensure ongoing compliance with KYC regulations.

5. Data Validation and Cross-Referencing:

- Employ ML to cross-reference and validate customer data against multiple sources for enhanced due diligence.

Results

Integrating AI and ML in KYC processes has significantly improved the efficiency and effectiveness of customer due diligence in banks. This approach has led to a reduction in compliance costs, faster customer onboarding, and enhanced detection of potential financial crimes. Banks leveraging these technologies have reported up to a 30% improvement in KYC compliance efficiency. The success of AI and ML in KYC hinges on the comprehensive and accurate analysis of customer data, continuous updating of risk profiles, and adherence to evolving regulatory standards.

AI-driven risk management in regional banks represents a substantial leap forward from traditional risk management practices. By leveraging the predictive power of ML and the broad analytical capabilities of AI, these banks can manage credit, market, operational, and compliance risks more effectively and efficiently. The case studies highlight the real-world benefits of these technologies, underscoring their potential to significantly enhance risk management strategies in the banking industry. As AI and ML technologies continue to evolve, they are set to play an increasingly vital role in shaping the future of risk management in regional banks.

Customer onboarding processes

Integrating machine learning (ML) and artificial intelligence (AI) into the customer onboarding process in banking revolutionizes how new clients are introduced to bank services. This technology-driven approach streamlines the onboarding process, making it faster, more accurate, and customer-friendly while ensuring compliance with regulatory standards.

Data Collection and Preparation

1. Personal Identification Data:

   - Source: Customer-submitted documents (ID proofs, application forms).
   - Content: Names, addresses, government-issued identification numbers.

2. Financial Background Data:

   - Source: Credit bureaus, previous banking records.
   - Content: Credit scores, financial history, existing liabilities.

3. Compliance-Related Data:

   - Source: Regulatory databases, watchlists.
   - Content: Information required for Know Your Customer (KYC) and Anti-Money Laundering (AML) checks.

4. Digital Interaction Data:

   - Source: Online form submissions, digital engagement platforms.
   - Content: Data input by customers during the digital onboarding process.

5. Feedback Data:

   - Source: Previous customer onboarding experiences.

- Content: Information about pain points, customer preferences, and areas for improvement in the onboarding process.

Model Development Logic

1. Document Verification:

- Use AI algorithms to verify the authenticity of documents and extract relevant information for KYC processes.

2. Risk Assessment:

- Implement ML models to assess the potential risk a new customer might pose, based on their financial history and compliance data.

3. Automated Account Setup:

- Develop systems that automatically set up new customer accounts and services based on verified information and customer preferences.

4. Personalization of Services:

- Use AI to analyze customer data and tailor banking services to suit individual needs and financial goals.

5. Compliance Checks:

- Integrate AI tools to ensure that all onboarding processes meet regulatory compliance standards automatically.

Results

The implementation of AI and ML in customer onboarding processes has led to significant enhancements in operational efficiency and customer satisfaction. Banks that have adopted this technology report reductions in onboarding time by up to 70% and improvements in customer satisfaction scores by up to 40%. Furthermore, these advanced systems have streamlined compliance adherence, reducing the risk of errors and ensuring more stringent KYC and AML practices. The success of these systems depends on the integration of accurate data sources, sophisticated ML algorithms, and a user-friendly interface that makes the onboarding experience more engaging for the customer.

Customer Service:

AI-driven chatbots and virtual assistants are handling customer queries, account information requests, and basic banking transactions. This automation improves customer service efficiency and availability while reducing the workload on human customer service teams.

Data Collection and Preparation
1. Source Documents:

- Source: Transaction forms, account opening documents, loan applications.
- Content: Includes personal customer information, financial details, transactional data.

2. Digital Forms and Records:

- Source: Online forms, digital transaction records.
- Content: Data entered by customers via online banking platforms or during digital transactions.

3. Historical Data Records:

- Source: Bank's archival database.
- Content: Historical banking records, previous transactional data.

4. External Data Sources:

- Source: Credit bureaus, public databases.
- Content: Supplementary customer information for credit assessments, background checks.

5. Regulatory and Compliance Data:

- Source: Compliance documents.
- Content: Information required for compliance with banking regulations.

Model Development Logic
1. Optical Character Recognition (OCR):

- Implement OCR technology to convert different types of documents (like scanned forms and handwritten notes) into machine-readable text.

2. Data Extraction and Classification:

- Use ML algorithms to extract relevant information from digitized documents and classify data into appropriate categories.

3. Validation and Verification:

- Employ ML models to cross-verify extracted data against existing databases for accuracy and consistency.

4. Automated Data Entry:

- Develop systems that automatically populate databases with verified and processed data, minimizing manual entry.

5. Error Detection and Correction:

- Integrate error detection mechanisms to identify and correct inaccuracies in data entry automatically.

Results

The incorporation of AI and ML in data entry processes within banks has led to substantial improvements in operational efficiency. For example, after implementing an AI-driven data entry system, a regional bank observed a 50% decrease in data processing time and a 30% reduction in data entry-related errors. These systems not only expedite the data entry process but also ensure higher accuracy, leading to better data quality. This, in turn, supports improved decision-making and regulatory compliance. The effectiveness of these systems is largely dependent on the sophistication of the OCR and ML algorithms used, the quality of the source data, and the integration of these systems into the bank's broader data management framework.

Transaction processing

Implementing machine learning (ML) and artificial intelligence (AI) in "Transaction Processing" within banking operations is aimed at automating and optimizing the handling of financial transactions. This innovation significantly enhances processing speed, accuracy, and security, offering a more efficient and reliable transaction experience for both the bank and its customers.

Data Collection and Preparation
1. Transaction Data:

- Source: Transaction processing systems, online and mobile banking platforms.
- Content: Includes details of customer transactions such as transfers, payments, deposits, and withdrawals.

2. Customer Account Information:

- Source: Bank's customer database.
- Content: Account numbers, customer profiles, historical transaction patterns.

3. Security and Fraud Data:

- Source: Security systems, fraud detection databases.
- Content: Information on previous security breaches, fraud attempts, and risk indicators.

4. Regulatory Compliance Data:

- Source: Compliance management systems.
- Content: Data related to anti-money laundering (AML), counter-terrorism financing, and other regulatory compliance requirements.

5. Real-Time Market Data:

- Source: Financial market data feeds.

- Content: Current market conditions affecting transaction validity, such as foreign exchange rates.

Model Development Logic

1. Automated Validation:

- Use ML algorithms to automatically validate transaction details against customer profiles and account information for authenticity.

2. Fraud Detection:

- Implement sophisticated ML models to analyze transaction patterns and flag anomalies that may indicate fraudulent activities.

3. Regulatory Compliance Checks:

- Automate compliance checks using AI algorithms to ensure all transactions adhere to regulatory standards, including AML and KYC (Know Your Customer) norms.

4. Real-Time Processing:

- Design systems to process transactions in real-time, thereby reducing the time gap between transaction initiation and completion.

5. Error Handling and Resolution:

- Integrate mechanisms for automatic detection and correction of transactional errors, minimizing manual intervention.

Results

The adoption of AI and ML in transaction processing has proven to be highly beneficial for banks. For instance, a regional bank implementing AI-based transaction processing systems reported a 40% improvement in transaction processing speed and a 60% reduction in transaction-related errors. Furthermore, the system enhanced fraud detection capabilities, leading to a significant decrease in fraudulent transaction instances. These improvements not only streamline the transaction process but also reinforce security and compliance, ultimately contributing to a more robust and customer-friendly banking environment. The success of these AI and ML applications depends on continuous data updating, algorithm refinement, and seamless integration with existing banking systems. AI systems can process transactions more efficiently than traditional methods. They can handle large volumes of transactions in real-time, ensuring speed and accuracy.

Chatbots for customer support

"Chatbots for Customer Support" in the banking sector involves implementing advanced machine learning (ML) and artificial intelligence (AI) technologies to automate and enhance customer service interactions. These AI-driven chatbots are designed to provide immediate, accurate responses to customer queries, improving service efficiency and customer satisfaction.

Data Collection and Preparation

1. Customer Interaction Data:

   - Source: Previous customer service records, digital communication logs.
   - Content: Includes customer inquiries, frequently asked questions, and common service requests.

2. Banking Product Information:

   - Source: Internal product databases and information systems.
   - Content: Details about banking products and services, terms and conditions, fees, and features.

3. Transactional Data:

   - Source: Transaction processing systems.
   - Content: Types and patterns of transactions typically queried by customers.

4. Natural Language Data:

   - Source: Customer interaction logs, social media, forums.
   - Content: Variations in customer language, colloquialisms, and phrasing of common questions.

5. Feedback and Survey Data:

   - Source: Customer feedback systems.
   - Content: Customer experiences, satisfaction levels, and areas for improvement in customer service.

1. Natural Language Processing (NLP):

- Implement NLP algorithms to enable the chatbot to understand and process customer queries phrased in natural language.

2. Intent Recognition and Classification:

- Use ML models to classify the intent behind customer queries, such as requesting balance information or reporting a lost card.

3. Automated Response Generation:

- Develop systems that generate accurate and relevant responses to customer inquiries based on recognized intent and available data.

4. Personalization:

- Tailor responses based on the customer's history and profile, offering a more personalized service experience.

5. Continuous Learning:

- Incorporate feedback loops, where the chatbot learns from each interaction to improve response accuracy and relevancy over time.

Results

The implementation of chatbots for customer support in banking has led to significant improvements in customer service efficiency and satisfaction. For instance, a regional bank reported a 40% reduction in average customer wait times and a 25% increase in first-contact resolution rates within the first three months of deploying a customer support chatbot. These AI-powered chatbots not only provide instant responses to routine queries but also free up human customer service representatives to handle more complex issues, enhancing overall service quality. Success in this area hinges on advanced NLP capabilities, continuous learning algorithms, and the integration of comprehensive, up-to-date banking knowledge bases.

Summary

AI is revolutionizing banking operations by automating routine tasks, processing transactions faster and more accurately, reducing costs and errors, and enabling efficient scaling. This is transforming regional banks into more efficient, agile, cost-effective, and customer-centric institutions. Banks leveraging AI for operational efficiency will be well-positioned to compete in the future of banking.

AI can analyze vast amounts of data, including historical financial data, market trends, and economic forecasts, to provide banks with a more comprehensive understanding of their risk profile. This allows them to make better-informed decisions about capital allocation and ensure they are holding sufficient capital to meet regulatory requirements and absorb potential losses.

Regulatory Compliance

The integration of machine learning (ML) and artificial intelligence (AI) in "Navigating Regulatory Compliance" in banking is a strategic approach to ensure adherence to financial regulations and laws efficiently and effectively. By leveraging these technologies, banks can automate and enhance the compliance process, reducing the risk of violations and associated penalties.

Data Collection and Preparation
1. Regulatory Requirements Data:

- Source: Regulatory bodies' publications, legal databases.
- Content: Current financial regulations, guidelines, compliance requirements (e.g., AML, KYC, GDPR).

2. Customer Transaction Data:

- Source: Bank's transactional systems.
- Content: Transaction details, patterns, anomalies indicative of suspicious activities.

3. Customer Identity and Verification Data:

- Source: KYC documentation, government databases.
- Content: Customer identification documents, biometric data, background check information.

4. Internal Policy Documents:

- Source: Bank's internal policy records.

151

- Content: Bank's compliance policies, procedures, and internal controls.

5. Audit Trails and Historical Compliance Data:

- Source: Previous audits, compliance reports.
- Content: Historical compliance issues, audit findings, remediation steps taken.

Model Development Logic

1. Compliance Monitoring:

- Use AI to continuously monitor transactions and customer activities against regulatory requirements, identifying potential compliance breaches.

2. Automated Reporting:

- Implement systems that automatically generate and submit necessary compliance reports to regulatory bodies, ensuring timely reporting.

3. Risk Assessment:

- Apply ML algorithms to assess the level of compliance risk associated with various transactions, customer profiles, and business activities.

4. Document Analysis:

- Utilize NLP techniques to analyze regulatory documents and updates, ensuring that the bank's policies remain aligned with the latest regulations.

5. Anomaly Detection:

- Employ ML models to detect anomalies in transaction patterns that might indicate money laundering, fraud, or other illegal activities.

The deployment of AI and ML in regulatory compliance has significantly enhanced banks' ability to navigate complex regulatory landscapes. For instance, banks utilizing these technologies have reported up to a 50% reduction in compliance-related operational costs and a notable decrease in compliance breaches. These systems not only ensure adherence to regulations but also streamline reporting processes and enhance the bank's ability to respond swiftly to regulatory changes. The effectiveness of these models depends on the continuous updating of regulatory data, the accuracy of the ML algorithms, and the seamless integration of these systems within the bank's broader operational framework.

Stress Testing and Scenario Planning

Incorporating machine learning (ML) and artificial intelligence (AI) in "Stress Testing and Scenario Planning" in banking has brought a significant shift in how financial institutions prepare for potential economic downturns and financial crises. These technologies enable banks to simulate various adverse scenarios more accurately and adapt their strategies accordingly.

Data Collection and Preparation

1. Economic and Financial Market Data:

   - Source: Financial markets, economic research databases.
   - Content: Historical market data, interest rates, stock indices, commodity prices.

2. Bank's Financial Data:

   - Source: Bank's internal records.
   - Content: Balance sheets, income statements, loan portfolios, investment holdings.

3. Regulatory Stress Test Scenarios:

   - Source: Central banks, regulatory bodies (e.g., Federal Reserve, European Central Bank).
   - Content: Prescribed economic scenarios, key variables, and indicators used in regulatory stress tests.

4. Customer Data:

   - Source: CRM systems, transaction databases.
   - Content: Borrower financial health, credit scores, default history, deposit behavior.

5. Operational Risk Data:

   - Source: Internal risk management reports.
   - Content: Operational losses, fraud incidents, IT system failures.

1. Scenario Generation:

- Utilize AI to generate a range of stress test scenarios, including extreme but plausible economic conditions.

2. Risk Assessment Models:

- Develop ML models to assess the impact of various stress scenarios on the bank's risk profile, particularly credit, market, and operational risks.

3. Capital and Liquidity Analysis:

- Apply predictive algorithms to estimate the bank's capital and liquidity levels under different stress conditions.

4. Portfolio Vulnerability Analysis:

- Use AI to analyze loan and investment portfolios, identifying areas of vulnerability in adverse economic environments.

5. Predictive Forecasting:

- Employ ML models for predictive forecasting of key financial metrics under stress scenarios, such as profitability, loan defaults, and market losses.

Results

The integration of AI and ML in stress testing and scenario planning allows banks to better anticipate potential financial challenges and develop more effective contingency plans. Banks utilizing these technologies have reported more robust risk management frameworks, with some achieving a more comprehensive understanding of their risk exposure, leading to more informed strategic decision-making. Success in this area is dependent on accurate and diverse data inputs, sophisticated modeling techniques, and the ability to interpret complex results for strategic planning.

Liquidity

Integrating machine learning (ML) and artificial intelligence (AI) in managing "Regulatory Liquidity" in banking is a progressive approach to ensuring financial stability and meeting regulatory requirements. These technologies provide advanced insights into cash flow forecasts, market conditions, and customer behavior, thereby enhancing liquidity management strategies.

Data Collection and Preparation
1. Cash Flow Data:

- Source: Bank's financial systems.
- Content: Daily cash inflows and outflows, including loan disbursements and deposit withdrawals.

2. Market Liquidity Data:

- Source: Financial markets, economic databases.
- Content: Market trends, interest rates, currency exchange rates, and economic indicators affecting liquidity.

3. Customer Transaction Data:

- Source: Transaction processing systems.
- Content: Customer deposit and withdrawal patterns, large transaction alerts.

4. Regulatory Requirements:

- Source: Regulatory bodies.
- Content: Liquidity coverage ratio (LCR), net stable funding ratio (NSFR), and other regulatory liquidity metrics.

5. Historical Liquidity Data:

- Source: Bank's financial archives.
- Content: Historical records of liquidity levels during various market conditions.

Model Development Logic
1. Cash Flow Forecasting:

- Employ ML algorithms to predict future cash flow trends based on historical data, identifying potential liquidity shortages.

2. Stress Testing:

- Conduct liquidity stress tests using AI models to simulate adverse market conditions and assess their impact on the bank's liquidity.

3. Customer Behavior Analysis:

- Utilize AI to analyze customer transaction patterns, forecasting future deposit and withdrawal behaviors.

4. Real-time Monitoring:

- Implement systems for real-time monitoring of liquidity metrics to promptly identify and address potential risks.

5. Optimization of Liquid Assets:

- Use AI to optimize the allocation of liquid assets, ensuring regulatory compliance and efficient use of resources.

Results

The adoption of AI and ML in liquidity risk management has led to enhanced predictive capabilities, improved regulatory compliance, and more efficient asset allocation. Banks leveraging these technologies report a more proactive approach to liquidity management, with some experiencing significant improvements in meeting liquidity requirements under various market scenarios. The effectiveness of these technologies depends on the accuracy of predictive models, the depth of market and transaction data analysis, and the integration of insights into liquidity management and planning strategies.

Consumer Protection Regulations

Incorporating machine learning (ML) and artificial intelligence (AI) in managing compliance with "Consumer Protection Regulations" represents a significant shift in how banks ensure adherence to laws designed to protect consumers. These technologies enable more efficient and accurate monitoring of compliance practices, better risk management, and enhanced customer service.

Data Collection and Preparation

1. Regulatory Guidelines Data:

- Source: Consumer protection agencies, regulatory bodies (e.g., CFPB, FDIC).
- Content: Current consumer protection laws, guidelines, and updates.

2. Customer Interaction Records:

- Source: Customer service databases, communication channels.
- Content: Call logs, emails, chat transcripts, complaint registers.

3. Transaction and Product Data:

- Source: Banking transaction systems, product management teams.
- Content: Details of financial products offered, transaction histories, fees and charges applied.

4. Customer Feedback and Surveys:

- Source: Customer feedback platforms, survey tools.
- Content: Customer satisfaction metrics, feedback on products and services.

5. Marketing and Sales Data:

- Source: Marketing departments, CRM systems.
- Content: Advertising materials, sales tactics, product promotion strategies.

Model Development Logic

1. Regulatory Change Management:

- Utilize AI systems to track and interpret new regulatory changes and updates in consumer protection laws.

2. Compliance Monitoring:

- Implement ML algorithms to monitor and analyze customer interactions, ensuring adherence to consumer protection standards.

3. Product Compliance Analysis:

- Use AI to review financial products and services for compliance with consumer protection regulations, including fair pricing and disclosure norms.

4. Customer Complaint Analysis:

- Apply ML techniques to analyze customer complaints, identifying trends and areas of non-compliance.

5. Risk Assessment Models:

- Develop risk models that evaluate and score the level of compliance risk associated with various bank practices and products.

Results

Adopting AI and ML in managing compliance with consumer protection regulations has enabled banks to maintain higher compliance standards and respond proactively to regulatory changes. This approach has led to more efficient compliance monitoring, improved customer relations, and reduced risk of legal penalties. Banks that have integrated these technologies report an improvement in their ability to detect and address compliance issues promptly. The success of these models depends on the continuous updating of regulatory data, accurate analysis of customer interactions, and the integration of compliance risk assessment into the bank's broader risk management strategy.

Gramm-Leach-Bliley Act (GLBA)

The integration of machine learning (ML) and artificial intelligence (AI) in ensuring data security and privacy compliance, particularly in relation to the Gramm-Leach-Bliley Act (GLBA), is a crucial development in the banking sector. These technologies enhance the ability of banks to protect customer data and maintain confidentiality, as mandated by GLBA.

Data Collection and Preparation

1. GLBA Compliance Requirements:

- Source: Legal and compliance departments, regulatory bodies.
- Content: Requirements for data protection, privacy notices, and safeguarding customer information.

2. Customer Personal Information:

- Source: Account opening forms, transaction records.
- Content: Names, addresses, social security numbers, financial data.

3. Data Access Logs:

- Source: IT systems, network logs.
- Content: Records of data access, modifications, and transfers.

4. Privacy Policy Documents:

- Source: Compliance and legal departments.
- Content: Bank's privacy policies, customer consent forms.

5. Third-party Vendor Information:

- Source: Vendor management systems.
- Content: Agreements with third parties handling customer information, compliance status.

Model Development Logic

1. Automated Compliance Monitoring:

- Use AI systems to continuously monitor compliance with GLBA data protection requirements across the bank's operations.

2. Customer Data Protection:

- Implement ML algorithms for the detection of unauthorized access or anomalies in customer data usage, enhancing data security.

3. Privacy Notice Management:

- Utilize AI to manage and automate the distribution of privacy notices to customers, ensuring compliance with GLBA's disclosure requirements.

4. Third-party Compliance Audits:

- Apply ML to assess and monitor third-party vendors for compliance with GLBA, ensuring the security of customer data.

5. Risk Assessment for Data Privacy:

- Develop risk models to identify potential vulnerabilities in data privacy and security, aligning with GLBA regulations.

Results

The application of AI and ML in GLBA compliance has significantly improved data security and privacy management in banks. These technologies allow for more effective monitoring of compliance, timely detection of security threats, and ensuring the confidentiality of customer information. Banks employing these technologies have reported enhanced data protection measures and adherence to GLBA standards, contributing to increased customer trust. The effectiveness of these systems depends on comprehensive data analysis, real-time monitoring capabilities, and alignment with the evolving landscape of data security regulations.

General Data Protection Regulation (GDPR)

Implementing machine learning (ML) and artificial intelligence (AI) to ensure compliance with the General Data Protection Regulation (GDPR) represents a significant advancement in data security and privacy management for banks. These technologies offer sophisticated solutions for protecting customer data, adhering to privacy norms, and managing consent effectively as required by GDPR.

Data Collection and Preparation
1. GDPR Compliance Guidelines:

   - Source: GDPR regulatory texts, legal counsel.
   - Content: Rules on data processing, rights of data subjects, data breach notification requirements.

2. Customer Personal Data:

   - Source: Account opening documents, digital banking platforms.
   - Content: Personal identifiers, contact information, financial transactions.

3. Consent Records:

   - Source: CRM systems, online banking portals.
   - Content: Documentation of customer consent for data processing, history of consent withdrawals.

4. Data Processing Activities:

   - Source: Internal data management systems.
   - Content: Data collection, storage, usage, and transfer records.

5. Data Breach Incident Logs:

   - Source: IT security systems.
   - Content: Records of data breaches, including affected data and remediation steps.

1. Automated Data Mapping and Inventory:

- Utilize AI to automatically map and classify personal data across the bank's systems, aiding in GDPR compliance.

2. Consent Management:

- Implement ML algorithms to manage and track customer consent, ensuring adherence to GDPR's consent requirements.

3. Data Subject Access Request (DSAR) Processing:

- Apply AI to efficiently handle DSARs, enabling customers to access, correct, or delete their personal data.

4. Anomaly Detection for Data Breaches:

- Use ML to monitor for unusual data access patterns, quickly identifying potential data breaches in line with GDPR's notification mandates.

5. Data Minimization and Retention Controls:

- Develop AI-driven systems to ensure data is not held beyond its necessary use, aligning with GDPR's data minimization principles.

Results

The integration of AI and ML in GDPR compliance has significantly strengthened data privacy and security practices in banks. These technologies enhance the ability to monitor and manage personal data responsibly, respond to customer data rights requests promptly, and detect potential data breaches swiftly. Banks leveraging AI and ML report increased efficiency in GDPR compliance, reduced risk of non-compliance penalties, and improved customer trust. The success of these initiatives hinges on the accurate mapping of data, effective management of consent, and the ability to adapt to the evolving interpretations and applications of GDPR.

AML Detection:

AI systems are particularly effective in detecting potential money laundering activities. By analyzing complex patterns of transactions that might elude manual detection, AI can flag suspicious activities for further investigation.

Implementing machine learning (ML) and artificial intelligence (AI) for Anti-Money Laundering (AML) detection is a strategic move for banks aiming to combat financial crimes effectively. These technologies offer advanced capabilities in identifying suspicious activities, thereby enhancing the efficacy of AML measures.

Data Collection and Preparation
1. Transaction Data:

- Source: Banking systems.
- Content: Details of customer transactions, including amounts, dates, locations, and frequencies.

2. Customer Profiles:

- Source: Account information databases.
- Content: Customer demographics, occupation, financial history, and risk categorization.

3. Suspicious Activity Reports (SARs):

- Source: AML monitoring systems.
- Content: Previously filed SARs, reasons for suspicion, outcomes of investigations.

4. Global Watchlists:

- Source: Government and international agencies.
- Content: Lists of individuals and entities involved in financial crimes.

5. Historical AML Cases:

- Source: AML department archives.

- Content: Records of past AML incidents, investigation notes, and patterns identified.

Model Development Logic

1. Anomaly Detection in Transactions:

- Utilize ML algorithms to identify unusual transaction patterns that deviate from typical customer behavior, indicating potential money laundering.

2. Risk Scoring:

- Implement AI-driven systems to assign risk scores to customers based on their transaction behaviors and profiles, aiding in prioritizing investigations.

3. Network Analysis:

- Apply AI to analyze relationships and connections between accounts, identifying complex money laundering schemes involving multiple parties.

4. Text Analysis of SARs:

- Use NLP techniques to analyze the text of SARs for common themes and indicators of money laundering.

5. Adaptive Learning:

- Develop models that adapt and learn from new patterns of money laundering, ensuring the AML system remains effective against evolving techniques.

Results

The use of AI and ML in AML detection allows banks to proactively identify and investigate suspicious activities with greater accuracy and efficiency. Banks employing these technologies have reported an enhanced ability to detect complex money laundering activities, leading to more effective prevention of financial crimes. The success of these models relies on comprehensive and quality data, continuous learning from new patterns, and the ability to integrate insights into AML operational workflows.

Predictive Risk Factor Analysis:

AI algorithms can predict potential compliance violations before they occur. By identifying risk factors and indicators of non-compliance, banks can proactively address issues, reducing the likelihood of regulatory breaches.

Leveraging machine learning (ML) and artificial intelligence (AI) for Predictive Risk Factor Analysis is an innovative approach for banks to anticipate and mitigate various risks. These technologies enable the identification and assessment of potential risk factors before they escalate into significant issues, thereby enhancing overall risk management strategies.

Data Collection and Preparation
1. Financial Market Data:

- Source: Financial market databases, economic research institutes.
- Content: Market trends, interest rates, stock prices, economic indicators.

2. Internal Bank Data:

- Source: Bank's transactional and operational systems.
- Content: Loan portfolios, investment data, deposit information, operational metrics.

3. Customer Data:

- Source: CRM systems, loan applications.
- Content: Credit histories, transaction behaviors, demographic information.

4. Regulatory Reports:

- Source: Regulatory filings, compliance departments.
- Content: Past regulatory compliance reports, findings from audits.

5. Historical Risk Data:

- Source: Bank's risk management archives.
- Content: Historical risk events, losses, previous risk assessments.

Model Development Logic

1. Credit Risk Analysis:

- Utilize ML algorithms to predict the likelihood of default by analyzing customer credit history, repayment patterns, and market conditions.

2. Market Risk Evaluation:

- Implement AI models to forecast market trends and assess the impact of market volatility on the bank's investment portfolio.

3. Operational Risk Assessment:

- Apply ML techniques to identify potential operational risks, such as system failures, process inefficiencies, or human errors.

4. Liquidity Risk Forecasting:

- Use AI to predict future cash flow scenarios and lIquidity needs, considering various market and operational factors.

5. Regulatory Compliance Prediction:

- Develop AI-driven systems to anticipate potential compliance issues based on emerging regulatory trends and internal data patterns.

Results

The adoption of AI and ML in Predictive Risk Factor Analysis allows banks to proactively identify and address risks, making informed decisions to mitigate potential impacts. This proactive approach has led to enhanced risk management, improved regulatory compliance, and optimized financial performance. Successful implementation depends on accurate data analysis, advanced predictive modeling, and the ability to integrate these insights into strategic risk management processes.

Know Your Customer (KYC) Due Diligence:

AI assists in the Know Your Customer (KYC) process and other due diligence measures, essential for AML compliance. It accelerates the verification process, enhances accuracy, and reduces the operational burden of compliance teams.

Implementing machine learning (ML) and artificial intelligence (AI) in the Know Your Customer (KYC) due diligence process represents a significant step forward for banks in enhancing customer verification, ensuring compliance, and preventing financial crimes. These technologies provide sophisticated solutions for accurately identifying customers, assessing their risk profiles, and monitoring ongoing relationships.

Data Collection and Preparation
1. Customer Identity Documents:

- Source: Account opening forms, digital onboarding platforms.
- Content: Government-issued IDs, passports, proof of address documents.

2. Transaction Data:

- Source: Banking transaction systems.
- Content: Account transactions, wire transfers, deposit patterns.

3. Customer Profiles:

- Source: CRM systems.
- Content: Customer demographics, occupation information, financial history.

4. Global Watchlists and Sanctions Lists:

- Source: Regulatory bodies, international databases.
- Content: Lists of politically exposed persons (PEPs), sanctioned entities, and individuals.

5. Historical KYC Records:

- Source: Bank's compliance archives.
- Content: Previous KYC checks, customer due diligence reports, risk assessments.

Model Development Logic

1. Automated Document Verification:

   - Utilize AI algorithms to authenticate identity documents and extract relevant information, ensuring accuracy in customer identification.

2. Risk Profiling:

   - Implement ML techniques to assess the risk associated with each customer based on transaction behaviors, associations with high-risk entities, and other risk indicators.

3. PEP and Sanctions Screening:

   - Apply AI to screen customers against global watchlists and sanctions lists, identifying potential compliance risks.

4. Behavioral Analysis:

   - Use ML models to analyze transaction patterns for signs of unusual or suspicious activity, flagging potential money laundering or terrorist financing.

5. Ongoing Monitoring:

   - Develop systems for continuous monitoring of customer activities using AI, ensuring ongoing compliance with KYC regulations.

Results:

AI has emerged as a transformative force in regulatory compliance within the banking sector. By automating compliance processes, enhancing the detection of AML activities, and providing predictive insights into potential violations, AI is enabling regional banks to meet their regulatory obligations more efficiently and effectively. The success stories illustrate the tangible benefits of AI in compliance, from cost savings and operational efficiency to improved accuracy and

171

real-time monitoring. As regulatory landscapes continue to evolve, AI technologies will be instrumental in helping banks navigate these changes, ensuring compliance, and safeguarding their reputation.

Chapter 10: AI on the Horizon in Regional Banking

As AI and ML technologies continue to evolve, their impact on regional banking is expected to grow significantly. This chapter explores key trends and future developments in AI and ML within the regional banking sector.

1. Greater Adoption and Sophistication:
   - Expect widespread adoption of AI and ML technologies, with applications becoming increasingly sophisticated.
   - Enhancements in predictive analytics and personalized banking services are particularly anticipated.
2. Focus on Ethical AI:
   - The development and deployment of AI will increasingly emphasize ethical considerations, including transparency and fairness.
   - Responsible AI practices will become a critical component of technology strategies in banking.
3. Collaboration and Innovation:
   - Collaborations between banks, fintech companies, and tech startups are likely to rise, fostering innovative solutions that could reshape the banking landscape.
4. Deep Learning:
   - Deep learning, known for processing complex data sets, will see expanded use in predictive analytics, risk assessment, and fraud detection in banking.
5. Natural Language Processing (NLP):
   - NLP will increasingly improve customer interactions, with advanced chatbots capable of handling complex queries and sentiment analysis from communication channels.
6. Blockchain and AI Integration:
   - The integration of blockchain with AI promises revolutionary changes in areas like secure payment processing and automated contractual agreements.

7. Advanced Data Analytics:
    - Enhanced data analytics methods will be key to extracting more accurate and actionable insights, crucial for AI-driven banking operations.
8. Edge Computing:
    - Edge computing will play a significant role, enabling faster and more secure transaction processing and customer interactions.
9. Hybrid Models:
    - Combining various AI and ML models to create hybrid systems can lead to improved performance and more comprehensive insights.
10. Bias Mitigation:
    - Addressing bias in AI algorithms will be essential to ensure fair and ethical decision-making in banking services.
11. Explainable AI:
    - The trend towards transparent and explainable AI systems will be significant, especially for applications in critical areas like credit assessment.
12. Regulatory Compliance:
    - Ensuring that AI systems comply with existing and emerging regulations will be paramount for banks.

Conclusion:

The future of AI and ML in regional banking is marked by greater sophistication, ethical considerations, collaborative innovation, and regulatory evolution. Banks must stay informed and adaptable to harness these technologies' full potential, ensuring they meet the changing needs of their customers and the industry. As AI continues to evolve, banks that effectively integrate these technologies while maintaining ethical and regulatory compliance will lead the way in the future of banking.

Synthetic Data in Banking

Synthetic data, artificially generated data that mimics real-world financial data, offers numerous advantages to banks, especially in areas of risk management, fraud detection, and regulatory compliance. Here are the key benefits:

1. Enhanced Privacy and Security:
    - **Data Anonymization:** Synthetic data doesn't contain real personal information, ensuring customer privacy and compliance with regulations like GDPR.
    - **Reduced Risk:** It minimizes the risk of data breaches, as it doesn't expose actual customer data.

2. Improved Model Training and Testing:
    - **Data Availability:** Banks can generate vast volumes of synthetic data for training ML models, particularly useful where real data is limited or sensitive.
    - **Overcoming Data Imbalance:** Synthetic data helps create balanced datasets for effective model training, essential in scenarios like fraud detection.

3. Regulatory Compliance and Testing:
    - **Stress Testing:** Enables banks to perform stress tests under various scenarios without relying on real transaction data.
    - **Compliance Testing:** Allows banks to test compliance with regulations without risking exposure of sensitive customer data.

4. Innovation and Product Development:
    - **Safe Environment for Innovation:** Facilitates experimentation with new technologies using synthetic data, mitigating risks associated with real customer data.
    - **Prototype Testing:** Ensures reliability and performance of new services or models before deployment.

5. Cost-Effective Solutions:

- **Reduced Costs:** Generating and using synthetic data can be more economical than managing large real datasets.
6. Enhanced Customer Experience:
   - **Personalization:** Develops models for personalized experiences without compromising customer privacy.
7. Global Reach and Scalability:
   - **Cross-Border Analysis:** Synthetic data can mimic data from different regions, enabling global analysis without regulatory hurdles of cross-border data transfer.
8. Risk Management:
   - **Scenario Analysis:** Facilitates creation of diverse scenarios for comprehensive risk assessment.

Importance of Comparing Synthetic Data to Real Data:

- **Accuracy Assessment:** Ensures the synthetic data generation process is accurate, assessing metrics like mean, variance, and distribution.
- **Data Quality Assurance:** Identifies biases or inconsistencies in synthetic data, confirming its reliability.
- **Model Performance Evaluation:** Trains models on synthetic and real data to validate the synthetic data's effectiveness.
- **Privacy Preservation Validation:** Confirms that synthetic data maintains privacy and doesn't contain sensitive information.

Methods for Comparing Synthetic Data to Real Data:

- **Statistical Analysis:** Employs techniques like hypothesis testing to assess similarity between distributions.
- **Visual Inspection:** Uses histograms and scatter plots for visual comparison of data distributions.
- **Machine Learning Evaluation:** Compares the performance of models trained on both types of data.
- **Domain Expert Review:** Involves expert assessment to spot inconsistencies or biases.

- **Privacy-Preserving Comparisons:** Utilizes methods like differential privacy for safe comparison.

Using Synthetic Data to Navigate Data Use Regulations in Banking

Synthetic data offers a strategic advantage to banks, especially in navigating the complex landscape of data use regulations while leveraging machine learning (ML). Here's how synthetic data is playing a crucial role:

1. Data Privacy and Compliance:
    - Synthetic data is created without using real customer data, thus aligning with data privacy regulations like GDPR and CCPA.
    - It's particularly beneficial in banking where customer data is highly sensitive and safeguarded.
2. Data Augmentation:
    - Synthetic data enhances existing datasets, improving ML model performance.
    - It can simulate rare or fraudulent events, aiding models in detecting such occurrences more accurately.
3. Testing and Validation:
    - It allows for rigorous testing and validation of ML models without exposing real customer data.
    - This step is crucial to ensure model accuracy and reliability before production deployment.
4. Data Sharing and Collaboration:
    - Banks can share synthetic data with others in the industry without compromising customer privacy.
    - Facilitates collaborative development of new ML models and applications.

Examples of Synthetic Data Applications in Banking:

- **Fraud Detection:** Training ML models to identify fraudulent transactions.

- **Credit Risk Assessment:** Enhancing credit lending decisions through ML models trained on synthetic data.
- **Customer Behavior Modeling:** Developing personalized products and services by understanding customer patterns through ML models.

Creating Synthetic Data: Key Steps

1. Define Data Requirements:
   - Determine the type, format, and size of the data needed.
2. Choose Generation Method:
   - **Sampling from a Distribution:** Generating data based on known statistical distributions.
   - **Fitting Real Data to a Distribution:** Creating a distribution model based on real data and then generating synthetic data from this model.
   - **Generative Adversarial Networks (GANs):** Using deep learning to generate data that closely mimics real data.
3. Validate the Data:
   - Ensure the synthetic data's accuracy and realism by comparing it with real data or using statistical tests.

Tools and Platforms for Synthetic Data Generation:

- **Mostly AI:** Offers capabilities to generate data from real datasets, fit distributions, and utilize GANs.
- **Synthetic Data Toolkit:** An open-source toolkit providing various synthetic data generation methods.
- **DataSynthesizer:** An open-source Python library for synthetic data generation.
- **Synthesize:** A commercial platform offering comprehensive synthetic data generation features.

Conclusion:

Synthetic data is becoming an invaluable tool in the banking sector, enabling banks to leverage ML's power while adhering to stringent privacy and data protection regulations. It facilitates innovation, model training, and testing, and collaboration in a secure and compliant manner. As the banking industry increasingly adopts ML, the role of synthetic data will continue to grow, driving advancements in banking services and operations.

Integrating Blockchain and AI technologies offers several significant benefits to banks, particularly in enhancing their operational efficiency, security, customer service, and compliance. Here are some of the key advantages:

1. Improved Security and Fraud Prevention:
   - Blockchain's decentralized and tamper-proof ledger provides an additional layer of security against data breaches and fraud.
   - AI can be used to analyze patterns and detect anomalies in transaction data, helping to identify and prevent fraudulent activities more effectively.
2. Enhanced Customer Experience:
   - AI can provide personalized financial advice and services based on customer data stored securely on a blockchain.
   - Smart contracts on blockchain can automate and expedite processes like loan approvals, reducing wait times for customers.
3. Operational Efficiency and Cost Reduction:
   - AI can optimize blockchain operations, making transactions faster and more cost-effective.
   - Automation of repetitive tasks and smart contracts can significantly reduce operational costs and improve efficiency.
4. Data Management and Analytics:
   - Blockchain provides a reliable source of data for AI algorithms, enhancing the accuracy of predictions and insights.
   - AI can analyze blockchain-stored data to provide actionable insights for decision-making and strategy formulation.
5. Regulatory Compliance and Transparency:

- Blockchain's transparent nature makes it easier for banks to comply with regulatory requirements, as transactions are traceable and immutable.
- AI can aid in monitoring and reporting, ensuring compliance with evolving regulations and standards.

6. Innovation and New Service Offerings:
   - The combination of AI and blockchain opens up opportunities for innovative financial products and services.
   - Banks can leverage these technologies to enter new markets or offer differentiated products, giving them a competitive edge.

7. Risk Management:
   - AI's predictive capabilities, when applied to the data integrity provided by blockchain, enhance the bank's ability to assess and manage risk.
   - This can lead to more informed lending decisions and better management of financial risks.

8. Enhanced Trust and Reputation:
   - Using advanced technologies like blockchain and AI can enhance a bank's reputation as an innovator and a secure institution.
   - Increased transparency and security can foster greater trust among customers and partners.

By integrating Blockchain and AI, banks can not only streamline their operations but also create a more secure, efficient, and customer-centric banking environment. This integration positions banks to better face the challenges of the digital era, including competition from fintech companies, evolving customer expectations, and stringent regulatory demands.

Where to start?

1. Define Objectives and Scope

Identify Needs: Determine specific areas where Blockchain and AI can add value (e.g., fraud detection, customer service, operational efficiency).

Set Goals: Define clear, measurable objectives for what the bank seeks to achieve with these technologies.

2. Conduct Feasibility Study

Assess Technical Feasibility: Evaluate the bank's existing IT infrastructure and its compatibility with Blockchain and AI technologies.

Financial Analysis: Analyze the costs versus benefits, including initial investment, operational costs, and expected ROI.

Risk Assessment: Identify potential risks and challenges associated with the integration.

3. Develop a Strategic Plan

Roadmap Development: Create a detailed roadmap outlining the phases of implementation, including timelines and milestones.

Resource Allocation: Allocate necessary resources, including budget, technology, and personnel.

4. Build or Enhance Technological Infrastructure

Infrastructure Upgrade: Upgrade existing IT systems to support Blockchain and AI functionalities.

Blockchain Platform Selection: Choose a blockchain platform that aligns with the bank's needs (e.g., Ethereum, Hyperledger).

AI Integration: Decide on AI tools and algorithms relevant to the bank's requirements.

5. Staff Training and Capacity Building

Skill Development: Train existing staff on Blockchain and AI technologies or hire new talent with the required expertise.

Change Management: Prepare the organization for change through effective communication and training programs.

6. Pilot Testing

Small-scale Implementation: Begin with a pilot project in a controlled environment to test the integration.

Monitoring and Feedback: Continuously monitor the pilot, gather feedback, and make necessary adjustments.

7. Compliance and Legal Considerations

Regulatory Compliance: Ensure that the integration complies with all relevant banking regulations and standards.

Legal Framework: Establish a legal framework to address any legal issues related to Blockchain and AI use.

8. Full-scale Implementation

Scalable Deployment: Gradually scale the solution across different departments and functions.

Integration with Existing Systems: Ensure seamless integration with existing banking systems and processes.

9. Continuous Improvement and Innovation

Monitor Performance: Regularly monitor the performance and impact of Blockchain and AI integration.

Iterative Improvements: Continuously improve the systems based on new technologies, feedback, and performance data.

10. Partnership and Collaboration

Collaborate with Tech Firms: Partner with technology companies specializing in Blockchain and AI for expertise and support.

Industry Collaboration: Engage with other banks and financial institutions to learn from their experiences and best practices.

Conclusion

Integrating Blockchain and AI is a complex but potentially transformative process for a bank. It requires careful planning, significant investment in technology and skills, and a willingness to innovate and adapt to new ways of operating. By following these steps, a bank can effectively harness the power of these technologies to improve efficiency, security, and customer service.

Appendix

Large Language Model, AKA Llama - An Overview:
Llama is a sophisticated artificial intelligence technology, categorized as a Large Language Model (LLM). It's engineered to comprehend and generate text in a manner that mirrors human communication, thus serving as an advanced AI tool for processing and producing language-based responses.

How Llama Functions:

1. **Trained on Extensive Data:** Llama's training encompasses a broad spectrum of text data, including financial literature, news articles, and general knowledge, equipping it to understand and engage with a variety of subject matters.
2. **Contextual Understanding:** In the dynamic banking environment, where context is key, Llama excels in grasping the nuances of a conversation or text input, providing relevant and coherent responses.
3. **Response Generation:** Llama generates responses based on its extensive training when posed with a question or task. It goes beyond mere retrieval of pre-existing answers, instead synthesizing responses from understood patterns and information.

Applications in Banking:

1. **Customer Service Support:** Llama enhances customer experience by providing quick and accurate responses to common banking inquiries.
2. **Financial Analysis and Reporting:** It assists in compiling financial reports, analyzing market trends, and delivering insights from substantial data volumes.
3. **Regulatory Compliance:** Llama aids in tracking regulatory changes and ensuring compliance through the summarization of complex regulatory documents.

4. **Risk Management:** Llama's analysis of financial data patterns and trends contributes to effective risk assessment and management strategies.

Benefits for Employees:

- **Efficiency Boost:** Automates routine tasks, enabling focus on more complex, strategic activities.
- **Enhanced Accuracy:** Reduces human error in data analysis and report generation.
- **Knowledge Resource:** Serves as a go-to reference for financial regulations, market trends, and banking products.

Limitations:

- **Not a Replacement for Human Judgment:** Despite its power, Llama does not substitute the nuanced decision-making and personal judgment of banking professionals.
- **Training Data Constraints:** Its efficacy and accuracy depend on the quality and recency of its training data, which may not always include the latest banking regulations or market updates.

In summary, for bank employees, Llama is a versatile AI tool that significantly streamlines banking processes, from customer service to compliance and risk management. Its use enhances productivity and decision-making, complementing rather than replacing human expertise.

Snowflake's Document AI: A Revolutionary AI-Powered Tool

Snowflake's Document AI is an innovative tool that leverages artificial intelligence to reveal hidden insights within organizational documents. Functioning like an advanced search engine, it understands both the keywords and the deeper meaning and context of documents.

Capabilities of Document AI:

1. **Transforming PDFs into Tables:** Effortlessly converts PDFs into structured data for analysis in Snowflake, eliminating manual data entry and the need for external tools.
2. **Extracting Key Information:** Skillfully pinpoints details like names, dates, amounts, and sentiments in documents, facilitating question-answering and deeper insights.
3. **Workflow Automation:** Integrates seamlessly into existing workflows, processing new documents as they arrive and saving time and resources.
4. **Productivity Enhancement:** Reduces the burden of manual document processing, freeing up time for more strategic tasks.
5. **Gaining a Competitive Edge:** Unlocks valuable information in documents, aiding in more informed decision-making and opportunity identification.

Early Users' Experiences:

- **Increased Efficiency:** A notable 90% reduction in invoice processing time.
- **Enhanced Decision-Making:** Extraction of customer sentiments from support tickets for faster issue resolution.
- **Opportunity Discovery:** Identification of trends in loan applications, spurring new product development.

Additional Features of Document AI:

- Powered by a specialized large language model for document understanding.
- Fully integrated into Snowflake's platform, complementing existing data and tools.
- Offers robust security and scalability, handling sensitive documents with reliability.

In conclusion, Snowflake's Document AI is a transformational AI tool that revolutionizes document handling and data extraction in organizations. Its integration into existing workflows, combined with its capabilities in data automation and analysis, makes it an invaluable asset for businesses aiming to boost efficiency and enhance decision-making.

Expanding on the Role of Large Language Models Like Snowflake's Document AI in Banking

Large Language Models (LLMs) such as Snowflake's Document AI play a vital role in the banking sector. Their ability to process extensive data, automate tasks, and improve customer interactions makes them essential in the competitive world of banking.

Cutting Edge Uses of Document AI:

1. **Improving Data Quality:** Identifies and corrects document errors and discrepancies, crucial for compliance management and report generation.
2. **Enhancing Customer Service:** Simplifies access to customer information for service representatives, leading to more efficient customer interactions.
3. **Democratizing Tribal Knowledge:** Captures and centralizes tribal knowledge, creating accessible and searchable repositories, and translating it into various languages for broader reach.
4. **Identifying Information Loss Risk:** Proactively secures knowledge at risk of being lost due to employee turnover.
5. **Reducing Technical Debt:** Supports code refactoring, generation, review, and automated testing, and educates developers about technical debt management.
6. **Streamlined Compliance:** Automates document collection and organization for audits, enhances the efficiency of audits, and ensures transparency in regulatory compliance.

Additional Advantages:

- **Workflow Automation:** Streamlines key banking processes, saving time and resources.
- **Risk Management:** Aids in early risk detection and strategic decision-making.

- **Market Analysis:** Processes market data to inform decision-making.
- **Customer Insights:** Analyzes customer feedback, informing service and product development.
- **Innovation in Services:** Leads to the development of new banking products and services.

In conclusion, Snowflake's Document AI, with its diverse applications, represents a significant advancement in banking technology. It streamlines various operations, enhances customer engagement, supports risk management, and fosters innovation, thereby maintaining a competitive edge for institutions.

Third Party LLM the Great Equalizer:
Large Language Models (LLMs) have emerged as transformative tools in the banking sector, especially for regional banks, democratizing access to advanced AI technologies and facilitating a range of operations and services.

Empowering Regional Banks with LLMs:

1. Enhancing Customer Interactions:
   - LLMs can significantly improve customer service and personalized marketing.
   - They provide AI-driven solutions that were once exclusive to larger banks, making sophisticated interactions more accessible.
2. Optimizing Operational Efficiency:
   - LLMs can streamline various banking operations, reducing the need for extensive resources and complex infrastructure.

Revolutionizing Data Exploration with LLMs:

1. Simplifying Data Access through Natural Language Interface:
   - LLMs can act as intermediaries between users and complex data sets, allowing for natural language queries and simplifying data access.

2. Data Summarization:
   - They can automatically summarize large datasets, highlighting key trends and insights efficiently.
3. Enhancing Data Exploration with Visualization Generation:
   - LLMs can create diverse visualizations, aiding users in understanding complex data relationships and patterns.
4. Interactive Exploration:
   - Enable interactive data exploration, where users can dynamically query and delve into specific data aspects.
5. Guiding Data Analysis and Identifying Anomalies:
   - LLMs can detect unusual patterns or outliers, crucial for in-depth analysis.
6. Generating Insights:
   - Capable of analyzing data and providing insights and explanations for observed trends.
7. Accessibility and Personalized Learning:
   - Tailor data exploration experiences to individual users' knowledge levels, enhancing accessibility.
8. Democratizing Data Science:
   - Empower non-technical users to perform basic data analysis tasks, broadening participation in knowledge creation.

Awareness of LLM Limitations:

- **Data Bias:** LLMs may inherit biases from their training data, leading to potentially misleading results.
- **Lack of Explainability:** Understanding the decision-making process of LLMs can be challenging.
- **Overdependence Risk:** Relying too heavily on LLMs might impede the development of analytical skills.

Summary:

LLMs offer a significant opportunity for regional banks to level the technological playing field. They can make advanced AI capabilities more accessible, enhancing customer interactions, operational efficiency, and data exploration. However, it's crucial to be aware of their limitations, including potential biases and the current challenges in explainability. As these models evolve, they hold the promise of becoming even more powerful tools for democratizing data access and enabling data-driven decision-making across all levels of expertise. Tailoring their use to the specific needs of each bank is key to successfully integrating and leveraging AI and ML technologies.

Strategies for Proofing and Monetizing Data in Banking
In the banking sector, where data is a key asset, it's crucial to understand how to prove the value of data and leverage it for monetization. Here are strategies that banks can employ:

Determining the Accounting Value of Data:

1. Intangible Asset Accounting:
    - Treat data as an intangible asset, with valuation based on acquisition, development, maintenance costs, and potential for revenue generation or cost savings.
2. Customer Lifetime Value (CLV) Estimation:
    - Use data to calculate CLV, offering insight into the long-term value of customer relationships.
3. Risk Assessment and Mitigation:
    - Quantify the role of data in risk assessment and mitigation, especially in critical areas like fraud detection.
4. Developing a Data Monetization Strategy:
    - Outline clear strategies on how data assets will be used for revenue generation or cost reduction as Chapterof financial planning.
5. Valuation Models:
    - Employ various valuation models like the income, market, or cost approach to estimate the value of data.
6. Legal and Compliance Considerations:
    - Ensure compliance with data privacy laws and regulatory frameworks in data valuation and accounting.
7. Transparent Reporting:
    - Report the value of data transparently to stakeholders, including shareholders, investors, and regulatory bodies.
8. Engaging External Experts:
    - Consult external experts for an objective valuation of data, ensuring accuracy and credibility.

Monetizing Data:

1. Data-Driven Products and Services:
   - Develop new banking products or services powered by data analytics, such as personalized financial advice or risk management tools.
2. Data Sharing and Collaboration:
   - Collaborate with fintech companies, research institutions, or other banks, sharing data in exchange for revenue or shared technological advancements.
3. Data Analysis Services:
   - Offer data analysis services to third parties, leveraging banking data insights to inform business strategies in other sectors.
4. Marketing and Personalization:
   - Utilize data for targeted marketing and personalized service offerings, increasing customer engagement and satisfaction.
5. Optimizing Operational Efficiency:
   - Use data analytics to streamline operations, reduce costs, and improve decision-making processes.
6. Creating Data Marketplaces:
   - Establish a marketplace for data where insights can be sold or traded, ensuring legal and ethical considerations are met.

Conclusion:

Proving and monetizing data in banking requires a multifaceted approach, combining accurate valuation, legal compliance, strategic monetization, and innovative use of data assets. By recognizing the intrinsic value of data and implementing effective strategies to leverage it, banks can unlock new revenue streams and enhance their competitive edge in the market.

AI Quick Start Guide for Beginners in Python

This guide is tailored for beginners interested in AI, focusing on using Python, SQL, and LLM (Large Language Models) for code generation.

Prerequisites:

- Basic knowledge of programming concepts.
- A computer with internet access.
- Python 3 installed.
- A SQL database management system (e.g., MySQL, PostgreSQL).

Tools:

- Python 3.
- SQL database management system.
- Optional: Jupyter Notebook for an interactive coding environment.
- LLM code generation tool (e.g., Bard, Copilot).

Steps:

1. Set Up Your Environment:
   - Install Python 3.
   - Install a SQL DBMS of your choice.
   - Optionally, install Jupyter Notebook.
   - Choose an LLM code generation tool like Bard or Copilot.
2. Practice Python Basics:
   - Start with basic Python concepts (variables, data types, operators, control flow).
   - Use online tutorials for beginners.
   - Write simple Python scripts.
   - Use LLM for generating basic code snippets.
3. Learn SQL Fundamentals:
   - Understand relational databases and SQL syntax.
   - Practice SQL queries: SELECT, INSERT, UPDATE, DELETE.

- Use online resources to learn SQL.
- Generate basic SQL queries with LLM tools.

4. Connect Python and SQL:
   - Install libraries (pandas, psycopg2) for database connections.
   - Learn to import data into Python (pandas DataFrames).
   - Use LLM for code generation related to database connections and data retrieval.

5. Practice Basic AI Concepts:
   - Learn about linear regression, logistic regression, decision trees.
   - Explore Scikit-learn and TensorFlow.
   - Use online tutorials for AI algorithms learning.
   - Generate code skeletons for these algorithms using LLM tools.

6. Build Simple AI Applications:
   - Combine Python, SQL, and basic AI knowledge to create applications.
   - Start with projects like customer behavior prediction.
   - Use LLM for code generation in specific project tasks.
   - Gradually increase project complexity.

Resources:

- Python Tutorials:
  - W3Schools Python
  - Learn Python
- SQL Tutorials:
  - W3Schools SQL
  - SQLBolt
- AI and ML Libraries:
  - Scikit-learn
  - TensorFlow
- LLM Code Generation Tools:

- Bard
- GitHub Copilot

Tips:

- Be patient and consistent.
- Utilize online forums for assistance.
- Start with simple projects, gradually increasing complexity.
- Use LLM tools as aids, not as substitutes for learning.
- Practice regularly.

Remember, the journey into AI is both exciting and rewarding. Stay curious and open to learning, and enjoy exploring the world of AI with Python and SQL!

Epilogue: Charting the Future of AI and ML in Regional Banking

As we conclude our deep dive into the integration of Artificial Intelligence (AI) and Machine Learning (ML) in regional banking, we stand on the cusp of a transformative era. The future beckons with a vision where AI and ML are not just auxiliary tools but fundamental drivers reshaping the banking landscape.

Encouraging Innovation in AI and ML:

1. Cultivating a Culture of Innovation:
   - Banks must prioritize fostering an environment that encourages experimentation and creative problem-solving.
   - Innovation transcends mere technological investments; it requires empowering the workforce to think innovatively and tackle challenges with novel solutions.
2. Collaboration and Partnerships:
   - Forming alliances with fintech startups, academic institutions, and technology firms can significantly boost innovation in AI and ML.
   - These partnerships are valuable for their fresh perspectives and specialized expertise, propelling forward-thinking and cutting-edge solutions in banking.
3. Investing in Research and Development:
   - A robust commitment to R&D in AI and ML is vital for sustaining growth and staying ahead in the competitive landscape.
   - Viewing R&D as a strategic investment, rather than a mere expenditure, is critical for the long-term viability and advancement of AI initiatives.
4. Learning from Other Industries:
   - The banking sector can extract valuable lessons from the application of AI and ML in other industries.
   - Cross-sectoral insights can reveal innovative applications and risk management strategies, which

can be adapted and applied within the banking context.

Fostering Continuous Learning in AI and ML:

1. Professional Development Programs:
   - As AI and ML evolve rapidly, ongoing training and development for banking professionals are essential.
   - Keeping pace with technological advancements in AI and ML is crucial for the effective management and application of these technologies.
2. Staying Abreast of Technological Advances:
   - Staying updated on the latest developments in AI and ML is imperative in this rapidly evolving field.
   - This includes keeping abreast of advancements in algorithms, data processing, and the development of ethical AI practices.
3. Promoting a Learning Mindset:
   - Encouraging a culture of curiosity and continuous learning is pivotal for fostering an agile and adaptable banking workforce.
   - A learning mindset is indispensable for leveraging AI and ML effectively and innovatively.
4. Engaging with Regulatory Developments:
   - Given the intricate relationship between AI/ML and regulatory compliance in banking, staying informed about regulatory changes is crucial.
   - Proactive engagement with policymakers and regulatory bodies is essential for strategic planning and effective risk management.

Closing Thoughts:

AI and ML are rapidly becoming integral to the banking industry, offering pathways to improved efficiency, enhanced customer service, and competitive strength. As these technologies continue to evolve, a focus on adaptability, ethical considerations, and continuous learning will be crucial for banks. With dedication to these principles, regional banks are well-positioned to navigate the transformative journey of AI and ML integration, poised to redefine the banking experience for their customers.

I encourage collaboration and am open to questions, suggestions, or discussions about potential partnerships, especially with youth in my home state of Mississippi. If you're interested in my work or would like to view some of my code developed in Python and SQL, please feel free to reach out to me at tim.h.heaton@gmail.com.

www.ingramcontent.com/pod-product-compliance
Lightning Source LLC
La Vergne TN
LVHW051330050326
832903LV00031B/3453